Using the environment
1 Early explorations

A Unit for teachers

Published for the Schools Council by
Macdonald Educational

A MACDONALD BOOK

© Schools Council Publications 1974

First published in Great Britain in 1974 by
MacDonald & Co (Publishers) Ltd

Maxwell House
74 Worship Street
London EC2A 2EN

A member of BPCC plc

Reprinted 1976 (with amendments), 1977, 1979, 1982, 1985

ISBN 0 356 04353 3

Library of Congress Catalog Card Number
77-83012

The author of this book is

Margaret Collis

The members of the Science 5/13 team were

Len Ennever	Project Director
Albert James	Deputy Project Director
Wynne Harlen	Evaluator

Roy Richards
Sheila Parker
Don Radford
Mary Horn

Made and printed in Great Britain by
Waterlow Ltd, Dunstable
A member of the BPCC Group

The Science 5/13 Project

'Science 5/13' is a Project sponsored jointly by the Schools Council, the Nuffield Foundation and the Scottish Education Department, and based at the University of Bristol School of Education. It aims at helping teachers to help children between the ages of five and thirteen years to learn science through first-hand experience using a variety of methods.

The Project produces books that comprise Units dealing with subject areas in which children are likely to conduct investigations. Some of these Units are supported by books of background information. The Units are linked by objectives that the Project team hopes children will attain through their work. The aims of the Project are explained in a general guide for teachers called *With objectives in mind*, which contains the Project's guide to Objectives for children learning science, reprinted at the back of each Unit.

Foreword

Margaret Collis has been a valued friend of the Science 5/13 Project since it began. It is entirely appropriate, therefore, that having written *Using the environment*, she should, with characteristic generosity, have made it part of the Project's materials.

For years before the Project even began she, I and others in the Project team had been working together on teachers' courses and on committees of various kinds, exploring child-centred ways of working in science and helping to introduce them into schools. Margaret Collis still works tirelessly with teachers of varied experience, and in the generous atmosphere she always creates, they respond with enthusiasm and conviction. She has become aware of their doubts and uncertainties, and having accumulated a great store of first-hand knowledge about what they really want to know, she offers them the advice they need and through it the confidence they seek.

Both knowledge and advice are now recorded in a book for teachers to keep by them and to consult year by year. It took many years to write, and it will be many more in active service.

L. F. Ennever
University of Bristol
1974

Acknowledgements

The Project is deeply grateful to its many friends: to the local education authorities who have helped us work in their areas, to those of their staff who, acting as area representatives, have borne the heavy brunt of administering our trials, and to the teachers, heads and wardens who have been generous without stint in working with their children on our materials. The books we have written drew substance from the work they did for us, and it was through their critical appraisal that our materials reached their present form. For guidance, we had our sponsors, our Consultative Committee and, for support, in all our working, the University of Bristol. To all of them, we acknowledge our many debts: their help has been invaluable.

It is a pleasure to acknowledge some further help of special value. Mr L. C. Comber, chairman of the Consultative Committee for the Science 5/13 Project and formerly HM Staff Inspector for Rural Studies read the first draft of *Using the environment.* His comments and suggestions have been of the greatest possible assistance in the work that followed.

Some of the apparatus photographed in Volume 3 has been constructed by Mr W. A. J. Edwards and Mr D. Postill, Kent Education Committee Inspectors. Mr Postill has also checked the sections in each book where there is emphasis on mathematical ideas.

Metrication

This has given us a great deal to think about. We have been given much good advice by well-informed friends, and we have consulted many reports by learned bodies. Following the advice and the reports wherever possible we have expressed quantities in metric units with Imperial units afterwards in square brackets if it seemed useful to state them so.

There are, however, some cases to which the recommendations are difficult to apply. For instance we have difficulty with units such as miles per hour (which has statutory force in this country) and with some Imperial units that are still in current use for common commodities and, as far as we know, liable to remain so for some time. In these cases we have tried to use our common sense, and, in order to make statements that are both accurate and helpful to teachers, we have quoted Imperial measures followed by the approximate metric equivalent in square brackets if it seemed sensible to give them.

Where we have quoted statements made by children, or given illustrations that are children's work, we have left unaltered the units in which the children worked—in any case some of these units were arbitrary.

Contents

Here we are walking down the road.

Introduction

This is a book about field studies. It deals with investigations and problems children can discover through their natural interest in their outdoor surroundings. Such first-hand experience, gained from the environment, is the basis of learning, provoking thought, giving children many ideas to share through speech and writing and sending them to books and other secondary sources of information to add to their own findings.

In the countryside there is so much more material of educational value than one book can cover that here there must be selection. We concern ourselves with things that have always interested scientists—natural phenomena that can be investigated through the human senses.

No rigid course with the same material for all is offered, that would fail to satisfy children's individual needs. When children work naturally they respond to the same starting points in different ways and soon become interested in different aspects of a common study. Later, as their development continues, they acquire the ability to make general statements about their experience or, as we usually say, 'form concepts', but here again, it is through varied experience that each child's understanding of ideas is consolidated and deepened.

Piaget and others have shown that children pass through the same stages of intellectual development in acquiring the power of conceptual thought, but there is nothing sudden about this maturing, it is something children come to at their own rate with frequent returns to earlier ways of thinking and working when new situations have to be faced. This means that we shall find children, even of the same age, at different stages in the way they learn from their surroundings, so teachers must be prepared to vary their influence correspondingly. For these reasons the material in this book is arranged in an order that can be related to children's changing needs as their experience of outdoor investigation increases.

Volume 1 is concerned with the earliest exploration beyond the classroom when children need experience that can sharpen their sensory perception and help them to think about the numerical and spatial aspects of their surroundings.

Usually this would apply to infants but older children, coming to field studies for the first time, will need some practice in early stages of the work before they become ready to deal with studies appropriate for more experienced investigators.

Volume 2 contains many questions and suggestions designed to help children work actively and purposefully on studies in depth. They become ready to do this when they find something of particular interest on which they wish to focus attention.

Volume 3 could serve as an impetus to early investigation of some major biological ideas and relationships through the design of controlled experiments. Children should be able to deal with the reasoning this involves as their capacity for abstract thought develops.

Volume 4 is relevant to fieldwork at all times. It deals with ways and means of providing the facilities, equipment and raw materials children need for all stages of their outdoor investigations and resulting activities on return to study areas in school.

A book concerned with the countryside should create awareness of the many ways in which living things and environmental conditions affect each other, so suggestions for studying these relationships and the consequences of disturbing them have been included. Every future citizen requires this knowledge as a basis for responsible attitudes towards the use of land and natural resources (ie *conservation*) in view of the ever-increasing demands a rising world population and desire for better standards of living will continue to make on the world's finite stores of materials.

Although this book is about children it is not for them; it is a book for teachers and it could not have been written without their help. Many teachers, and in particular some in Derbyshire and Kent, have contributed directly or indirectly to its contents. They have done so by encouraging children to pursue scientific interests, share common experiences and record what seems significant to them. They have collected questions children have asked, described models they have designed and noted suggestions and problems that have absorbed their attention. In this way a large collection of ideas has emerged from children's purposeful activity, guided carefully by thoughtful teachers. This is now available as a source of inspiration from which other teachers can select when children they know, show by their questions and behaviour that they are near the end of their own ideas and resources and need contact with the greater experience of an interested adult.

What's happening over there?

1 Beginning—beyond the classroom

Finding the first objectives

One of the first questions asked by many teachers wishing to make more use of the outdoor environment is 'How shall we begin?'

The most obvious suggestion children and teachers can agree to follow is 'Let's go out and see what's there'; for some general looking and probing around is necessary if children are to have opportunities of discovering what really is there and so be in a position to choose their own investigations.

Some children soon find something they wish to know more about. Teachers, by withholding their own suggestions, encourage these children to think of their own ways of developing their work yet help them through consultation and by anticipating the materials and apparatus they may require. Skilful classroom organisation makes it possible for different investigations to proceed alongside each other. In these circumstances much original, exciting work develops. Other children think more slowly and for some time need leading questions and suggestions from their teachers before they become fully alive to what their surroundings can offer. There are also many other children, and their teachers, whose interest declines steadily after the first excitement of 'going out' has passed. This happens when the first expedition is merely an unplanned attack on the countryside instead of a thoughtful investigation of its possibilities. Then material brought back to the classroom for no particular reason finds it way to the wastepaper basket or gathers dust as it lies neglected on the Nature Table.

Obviously teachers at a loss cannot help children

needing support. 'Let's go out and see what's there' is certainly a good suggestion to make to children but many teachers may find it too vague. For them a better approach would be to remember that children's knowledge and understanding of ideas develop gradually as they do their own thinking about experiences that come their way, so it may be better to ask 'What are some of the experiences that may sharpen children's awareness of their outdoor surroundings and how can we encourage them to wonder about what they observe?' This question always provokes vigorous discussion when teachers meet and the following suggestions are some that emerge most frequently.

1. *Investigating at different levels and in many directions*—Too often attention is concentrated at eye level and many things on the ground and in the sky are missed.

2. *Using the other senses as a means of collecting information*—Looking is not the only way.

3. *Developing a natural interest in making and arranging collections*—Through this many plants, animals and materials can be studied and sorted into classes (or sets).

4. *Making comparisons by measuring and testing*—Then children find interests to follow and problems to solve.

5. *Making observations about numerical and spatial aspects of the environment*—There must always be a close partnership between mathematics and science. Things that attract children's attention occur in different quantities, occupy different positions and alter in size and proportion. Statements about investigations become much more significant when they can be expressed in

quantitative terms. In this way mathematics is an aid to scientific observation. At the same time, children will often find, through their scientific interests, genuine reasons for using mathematical ideas and calculations, and in this way gain deeper understanding of what they are doing than through the working of pages of sums set as meaningless exercises.

6. *Finding appropriate words to describe experience*— This is the right basis for developing knowledge of language, and attempts to express thoughts in words can increase understanding. Although there is no section specifically devoted to this, the theme runs right through everything that is discussed.

Words and writing linked with the growth of a plant in an infant school

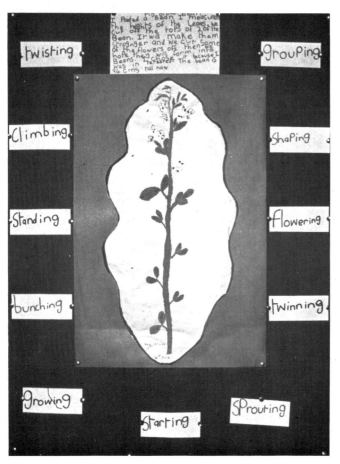

Achieving the first objectives

Any outdoor surroundings can offer children the experiences already listed but the extent to which this may lead to thinking and learning is another matter. This was a question that arose on one occasion when a small gipsy girl was seen playing on the grass verge of a busy trunk road. She used a large black puddle and containers from the scrap debris around her to give herself all the experiences with water that many infant children enjoy regularly in the hygienic settings of modern well-equipped classrooms. Yet how far will a little girl playing in this way *think about* the scientific and mathematical ideas that can be met naturally on any roadside or by any puddle if the help of a more experienced adult is always lacking ? On any fine August holiday afternoon it is equally easy to find busy self-employed children and aimless wanderers on waste land or commons where trees, logs, wild flowers and a mill pond or stream can offer many interesting starting points. It is also true that many mothers are relieved when the long summer holidays come to an end.

There is therefore evidence for thinking that many children, at different times, do reach the end of their own resources and need help—not the domination of a leader who treats the environment as an animated visual aid and conscientiously points out its features to her passive victims but an interested companion ready to co-operate when required.

It is through *conversation* and *discussion* with a more experienced person, aware of their needs, that children find inspiration for doing more with their surroundings. The art of talking *with* children is one that has to be cultivated. We have all heard the dutiful infant class choruses of 'Ye-es' and 'No-o-o' produced by some conscientious questioners. Such responses do not come from active, individual thought, they are merely children's attempts to give their teacher what they think she wants. Obviously, if a teacher asks a large group a question where a direct affirmative or negative will meet the case that is just what she will get—that approach is restricting. Much more individual treatment is required if each child is to be encouraged to extend his use of language through spontaneous chatter and so reveal what he is really interested in doing and thinking. It is easy to interest children in new names when these can be given to things as they are discovered. They enjoy collecting good words for describing new sensations and observations such as the feel of mud squelching and oozing around wellingtons or the sound of a noisy milk-bottling machine which, as one six-year-old said, 'went bang, thud, boom, clink, clank, crash, whiz, whirr, whine, hum, ring, rattle.' Children will soon respond to adults who know when to be quiet and listen, who can encourage, draw attention to exciting things which are being overlooked and offer suggestions when it is difficult to decide how an investigation should continue.

What about the teacher's own resources for this role of guide and helper? She can prepare by increasing her own knowledge of interesting places children can visit and by enlarging the store of ideas in her own mind about outdoor activities and further investigations that may arise as a result of these explorations on return to school.

Looking upwards and downwards

2 Ideas for conversation and experience

Learning to look

All around
1. Good explorers must learn to look everywhere. Where can we direct our eyes?

A chart can be made for recording the results of looking in different directions and at different levels (to be completed by sticking on drawings or listing words).

Looking in the Playground			
In front	Behind	Upward	Downward
gate railings road crane	school door windows	clouds birds	grass stones tarmac

At a later stage similar charts can be made in different places and the children's observations associated with compass directions.

2. 'I spy' games.

a. 'I spy' on my way to school.

A page from the diary of a ten-year-old boy of low ability showing how he has developed the habit of noticing interesting things around him due to his teacher's encouragement

> Friday June 24th
> Last night it rained and I stayed in and watched two house martins building there nest. This morning I saw a Jackdaw sitting on our fence. There is a S.W wind today. This morning the grass is wet and I saw a spider carrying its egg in his jaws and it carried it right over a puddle. It streched its legs and put its head with its egg in its mouth and swam across.

I spy, on my way to school,

Sarah
I spied a birds nest on the way home.

I spied a caterpillar on the way to school on a willow tree

mrs crosse Found this caterpillar galloping across the road

I spy on the way to school I saw a red poppy Michelle

Tracy
on the way to school I spied a little bird and it had hurt its wing so I took it home to my mummy and my mummy said she would take it to the Vet

I spied a ladybird and it was on a plant and I was going to bring it to school on Monday but it flew away

Lisa K

I spied a Flood on the way home from school it was raining
Michel

The photograph above is an example of some work which appeared in a large class book in an infant school. The children contributed to this book each day by recording observations of what they had seen on their way between home and school.

b. 'I spy' during walks with class teacher.

Urban
To the railway station
In shop windows
In the market
In the park
On the waste ground
From the bridge

Rural
Along the lane
By the stream
Around the village
In the wood
On the farm
By the pond

7

Concentrating on looking upwards

1. What is up there today? (Sky, clouds, sun, birds, smoke, chimneys, TV aerials, trees, roofs, aeroplane.)

2. What colours seem to be in the sky today?

3. Is it like that every day? What shall we do to find out?

4. Are there any clouds? How many?

5. What are they like?

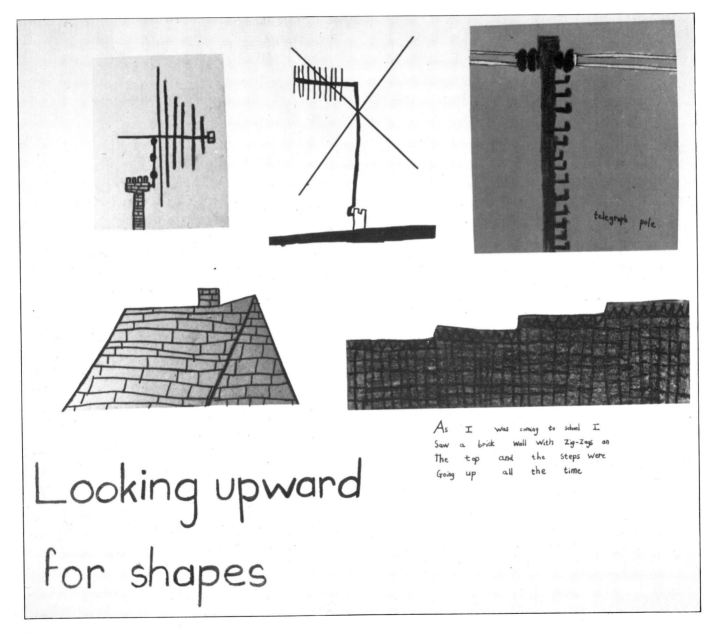

telegraph pole

As I was coming to school I
saw a brick wall with zig-zags on
the top and the steps were
going up all the time

Looking upward
for shapes

6. How much of the sky do they cover?

7. Do they seem to be high or low?

8. Are they moving much?

9. Have you ever tried to draw or paint a cloud?

10. What can we do to find out whether the sky changes:

At different times on the same day?
At the same time on different days?
When the sun sets?

11. I wonder how many different kinds of clouds you can manage to see this week. Pictures of clouds should be available for reference while this investigation is in progress. See *Instant Weather Forecasting* by Alan Watts (Rupert Hart-Davis, 1968).

12. Can you see anything moving above you:

Right across the sky?
Up and up into the sky?
Yet staying in the same place?

13. Do some moving things travel across the sky more quickly than others? What could you do to find out?

14. When do the leaves on the trees shake very much? Do some leaves shake more than others:

On the same tree?
On different trees?
On the bushes?
On plants near the ground?

15. When does the smoke go straight upwards?

16. What happens to the smoke when it doesn't go straight upwards?

17. What happens to our wind sock:

When the leaves are shaking hard?
When the smoke from the chimney goes straight upward?
When the clouds are scudding across the sky?
When the weathercock faces south?

(Attempt to get children to connect one observation with another.)

How are they moving?	Smoke	Leaves	Wind sock	Clouds across the sky	Wind from
Monday	Straight up	Almost still	Drooping	Still	South
Tuesday		Shaking gently	Fluttering	8 minutes	South-west
Wednesday	Blown away	Shaking hard		4 minutes	South-west
Thursday					
Friday					

18. What is the sky like when it rains?

19. Can raindrops be seen when they fall? What are they like?

20. Do they fall straight downwards?

21. What happens to raindrops when they fall:

On to flat roofs?
On to sloping roofs?
On to the window-pane?
Into a puddle?
On to a flower bed?
On the hard playground?
On to your mackintosh?

22. Can you find a way of making water fall like a shower of rain? (Provide a watering can.)

Leaves after rain

Making a shower

Making water travel

23. Can you make a stream of water come out of a squeezy bottle like the one that comes out of a garden hose? (A scent spray or water pistol can also be used.) How can you make the stream from your bottle travel a long way or a little way before it falls downwards?

24. What happens to your stream of water if you force it to go upwards?

25. If you let your rain shower and your stream from the bottle fall on your hand do they feel different?

26. Can you get a drop of water to rest on something? (Provide a dropper.)

Collect materials a drop of water will/will not rest upon. Can you make large and small drops with your dropper? Are they all the same shape?

27. What about collecting some rainwater?

How could we do that?

28. I wonder whether rainwater is different from other kinds of water.

29. Could we make a collection of different kinds of water, from a puddle, stream or pond, hot tap, cold tap, boiled water, or purified water from the chemist?

30. What can we do to find out whether these waters are different?

Look.
Look through.
Smell.
Feel and wash hands with and without soap.
Taste selected specimens (distilled, tap) under supervision of teacher.
Shake up, filter and see what the filter paper catches.
Allow same amounts to dry up.

Investigating water from different places by smelling, filtering and shaking with soap flakes

Shake up with same amount of soap flakes.
Put similar-sized groundsel plants in each type of water
and see how long they live.

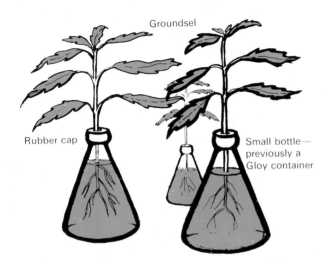

Groundsel

Rubber cap

Small bottle—
previously a
Gloy container

Drawing the caretaker's house

31. What shape is the roof of that house? (Point to the sloping roof of the caretaker's house.)

32. Does the roof look the same on each side? Can anybody make a drawing of it?

33. What stops the gutter of the house becoming full and overflowing when it rains?

34. Where does rainwater go when it leaves the gutter?

35. What are roofs of houses made of?

36. Could we make a collection of materials used for making roofs of houses?

37. I wonder which is the strongest material. What could we do to find out?

38. What does the roof keep out of the house? (Rainwater, light.)

39. It would be a good idea to make collections of things that let water and light in and those that keep them out. An example is shown on the right.

Material	Rain	Light
Slate	Out	Out
Tile	Out	Out
Wood	Out	Out
Velvet	In	Out
Rubber	Out	Out
Glass	Out	In
Perspex	Out	In

40. I wonder whether any more of the materials listed on the chart would let water through if we went on testing for a longer time.

41. A vocabulary list relating to the testing of materials as suggested in 39 can be made eg:

dark
light
thin
thick
transparent
opaque
waterproof
permeable

42. If you get a chance of watching a man putting tiles on the roof of a house can you discover exactly what he does? Where does he begin? In which direction does he work? Do the tiles overlap in the same way as a fish's scales? Where can we find other things that overlap in much the same way?

43. I wonder what holds up the roof of a house. Shall we go for a walk round the new estate they are building and try to find out?

44. Do the biggest houses have the most chimneys?

45. I wonder who can find different kinds of chimneys on the way to school or when out with father and

On the building site

mother. I should like a drawing of any you see. (A frieze with drawings and pictures of chimneys may be constructed.)

Chimneys in Chatham

46. It's so sunny today that we must put on sunglasses for looking around. How does this alter things you look at? Can we find any other glasses to look through? Convex and concave lenses, a block of glass, sheets of coloured cellophane can be provided.

47. If you stand on a mark in the playground and look through your sunglasses at your shadow every hour do you look in the same or different directions? What about trying to do this?

48. *Never* look straight at the sun through a telescope; it will hurt your eyes. If you place a piece of tissue paper on the playground and let the sun's rays come through a glass on to it you will soon see how strong the sun's rays are.

49. If you stand under a tree and look upwards when the sun is shining what can you see (in summer when the tree is in leaf)?

50. How do the leaves all manage to get some light from the sun?

51. Shall we try to borrow some binoculars or make a telescope and see what happens when we look around with them? (For instructions for making a telescope see James, A., *Simple Science Experiments*, page 29, Schofield and Sims, 1964.)

52. Who would like to take the telescope home and look up at the sky when it is dark? We could make a chart about all the things you see.

Can I use the sun to make it burn?

Children's contributions to a chart in an infant school

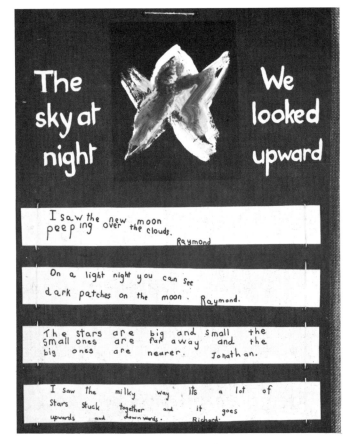

14

53. When children have opportunities of becoming interested in the colours of the spectrum, as, for example, when simultaneous showers and sunshine cause rainbows, follow up by encouraging them to search for similar arrangements of colours:

In prisms.
At the edges of mirrors.
On drops of water from the garden hose when the sun is shining.

54. If you watch a bird or aeroplane moving further and further away what seems to happen to it? (See page 52 no. 7, for further suggestions about investigating this illusion.)

55. Are all the TV aerials in the road alike?

56. Do birds perch on TV aerials? On what other things do they like to perch? What do they do while they are perching? (Attempt to help children to become aware of birds' use of song perches.)

57. I wonder who can find some good patterns against the sky. Winter is a good time for this, when bare trees, pylons, telegraph wires, etc, can be observed and drawn.

Concentrating on looking downwards
1. It might be interesting to explore the ground today.

2. I wonder how many different kinds of ground surfaces we shall manage to find.

3. Can you stand on all kinds of ground? I wonder why not.

4. If you stamp hard on as many ground surfaces as you can find do you get the same kinds of sounds? Are any of these sounds louder than others?

5. What sort of ground feels very soft?

6. It might be a good idea to make a collection of things we can find on the ground. (The collection might consist of stones, rocks, soils, materials, plants and small animals; and drawings of items that cannot be collected, eg a puddle.)

7. Why must we all wash our hands carefully when we have finished this job?

8. Who keeps the road clean? How does he keep his hands clean?

9. You could try touching things when you wear rubber gloves and noticing what your hands are like afterwards.

10. Can you find some things that will/will not allow dirt (soil) to pass through? (Strainers, net, a colander, papers can be tested.)

11. How did the big puddle in the playground get there?

12. What happens to water when we don't put it into something?

13. I wonder how many things we can find that:

Let water pass through them.
Hold water.

14. Provide a collection of bottles of different shapes and sizes.

Which bottle holds the most water?
Can you stand the bottles in order when you have found out how much each one can hold?

15. What happens to water from the smallest bottle if you pour it into the biggest?

16. How many bottles can you fill with all the water the biggest one holds?

17. How many shapes can you make the same water become by pouring it into different things? Could you make a collection of drawings of these shapes? (See page 54, nos. 9 and 10.)

18. I wonder whether this puddle will always be the same size. What could we do to find out? (Mark its edge daily.)

19. If you stand over a puddle and look into it what can you see? (A reflection.)

20. If somebody makes the water move do the reflections there change in any way?

21. How many other things can you find in which you see yourself?

22. Can you write about your discoveries on our chart?

Where can you see a reflection?

Pauline Kemp
In a picture in a book

Michael Watling
My self in the shiny side of our car.

Carol Dunn
Myself in our shiny table.

Colin Beal.
Things in the shiny jugs.

Jane Wilks
Reflections in my shiny shoes

Caroline Allwood
The room on the window glass at night.

Michael Watling
Me in the mirror.

Patricia Staples
Reflections on the shiny floor.

Michael Watling
I saw a reflection of Mrs Hobleys table in the glass cupboard

Christine Bligh
I saw a reflection of the trees in the puddle.

Mark Watts
When you are close to some one you can see your reflection in their eyes

David Harris
I saw a reflection in a pool it was me.

Hilary Stocking
I saw my reflection in Keston Pond.

23. Who would like to divide the materials you have collected into those that give reflections and those that do not? (Experience of shiny and dull.)

24. Can you find any good ways of fixing some mirrors together so that they stand up and allow you to see yourself? (Provide small handbag mirrors and Sellotape.)

25. How do you know there has been a puddle after it has dried up? (Silt remains.)

26. I wonder whether we can find anything by drying up different kinds of water (tap, sea, from a puddle, distilled, etc).

Discussion

How can we carry out a fair test? Put the same amount of each type of water (two teaspoons) in similar containers. Small watch glasses are suitable as contents are well exposed and dry up quickly; the sediment remaining is easily visible.

27. How can we make this sort of drying up happen quickly?

Demonstration of evaporation by teacher
Evaporate salty water with a spirit lamp or Gaz burner.

Where could we put water to see if the times taken to dry up are different?

From children's suggestions

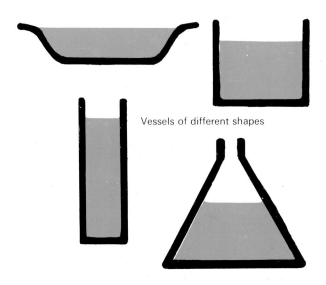

Vessels of different shapes

How much water in each vessel? (Same amount.)

Where shall we get the water? (Same place.)

Where shall we stand the vessels? (Same place.)

Who dries things very often? (Mother on washing day.)

What about a washday in the Home Corner to see if we can find out more about drying? Note time dolls' clothes and bedding take to dry.

Discussion
Was this test on drying a fair one? Were the things we dried of different sizes and made of different materials?

Better tests
a. Same materials of the same size hung or placed in the following ways:

Folded in halves.
Screwed up.
Pegged flat.
In a windy place.

Where it keeps still.
In the shade.
In sunshine.
Near a radiator.

b. Different materials of the same size hung in the same conditions.

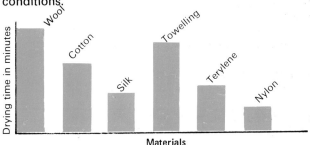

28. Who would like to know another way of getting things out of water?

Demonstration of filtering by teacher
Who would like to find different substances to stir with water for filtering?

29. What happens to the fine soil left by a puddle when it gets very dry? Can you draw the pattern made? (Cracks in dry mud.)

30. What does this fine soil feel like:

When it is dry?
When it is wet?

Vocabulary
Smooth, silky, sticky, dry, wet.

31. I wonder whether soil is made of different-sized bits. Would you like to try to find out? Shall we put some under the magnifier?

Collect old household strainers with different-sized meshes and show children how to rub dry soil through them with a wooden spoon. Encourage them to sort soils into different heaps according to the size of the particles.

32. It would be interesting to try to make an egg timer. If I give you some different sands you can find out which one will be best for it. Who can discover the best size to make the hole in the card between the two parts of the egg timer? How much sand shall we use?

Two Gloy bottles

Piece of card with small hole, cut to size and bind with sellotape

Silver sand

33. What sort of soil sinks to the bottom of water first?

Children could shake up about a teacup of soil in an old gas jar of water, leave it for twenty-four hours and then measure the different layers that have settled.

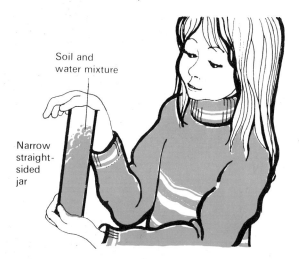

Soil and water mixture

Narrow straight-sided jar

34. What sort of soil does the gardener like for growing his seeds? Perhaps you could find out if you watch your father making his seed bed.

35. Can you discover why there are puddles in the playground after rain but not on flower beds and the lawn?

36. In the Discovery Corner I will put out some things that you can use for finding out more about liquids running through things. Notice the time your tests take.

Materials for this investigation:

Solids	**Liquids**
Sand	Water
Fine silt	Olive oil
Clay	Vinegar
Chalky soil	
Salt	

Can you find some materials that water will run through?

37. Let's just stop for a minute and look at a path. Does it seem to be the same size all the way along? Now you can test what you think by measuring with a plastic rope. (Connect with ideas on page 52, no. 7.)

38. What about looking for different stones today? How many colours can you discover in them? You could set them out on the Nature Table and put the names of their colours by them. (Egg or fruit trays are useful for keeping collections spaced and orderly.)

39. Do you know what gems are and what is done to them to make their beautiful colours show?

You might like to see if you can find something in the Book Corner about this.

Pictures of gems can be obtained from the British Museum (Natural History), Cromwell Road, London SW7.

Visits could be made to see gems at:

The Tower of London.
British Museum (Natural History), Geological Gallery, Cromwell Road, London SW7
Institute of Geological Sciences Museum, Exhibition Road, London SW7

40. Why do you think colours are mixed in some stones?

41. I wonder how many stones of different sizes you can find.

42. If you find two stones that seem to be the same size can you think of any way of finding out whether one is really bigger than the other? (By weighing and by displacement of water in measuring cylinder; see page 54, no. 11.)

43. I wonder who can find the heaviest stone; the lightest stone.

44. Who can find things on the ground that are: heavy and small, or large and heavy, or large and light? Can you arrange your stones in order from heaviest to lightest?

45. Shall we make a word list about our stones? (Round,

oval, smooth, white, sharp, pointed, big, small, names of colours, irregular, broken, etc.)

46. Can you find any broken stones? In how many ways can a stone be broken in halves?

47. Can you make your finger go round the edge of one of your broken stones? Now rub your finger over the flat part of the stone that is not the edge.

Discuss the difference between perimeter and area.

48. Can you place the flat part of your stone on a sheet of paper and draw round it?

49. Is there anything you can say or write about the shape you have drawn? Can you find broken stones now that give you different shapes?

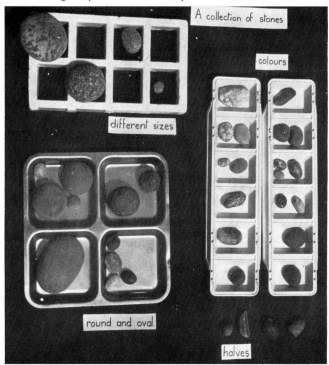
Sorting a collection of stones

50. Some shapes have names. Do you know any of these names? (Circle, oval, triangle, rectangle, square, parallelogram.)

51. It might be interesting to make a collection of materials people have used for building walls: flints, rocks, bricks, concrete, breeze blocks, reconditioned bricks, etc.

I wonder how the builder decides what to use.

What can you discover about the size of a brick?

You could try to discover different ways in which builders arrange the materials they put in their walls.

You could try to draw the patterns the bricks make and we could put your patterns in a class book.

How could we discover the strongest arrangement for making a wall?

Discussion of a suitable test
Make small brick-shaped blocks of clay, plaster of Paris, expanded polystyrene or balsa wood. Stick them together to form walls with different arrangements of blocks. Test for breaking strain by pulling, bending, pressing, etc.

How do we make sure we test each of these walls in the same way?

If you could collect a lot of sugar cartons to represent bricks, you could build a wall to shut off part of the room as a Home Corner.

52. Can anybody find any patterns made by things pressing into the ground?

53. Where can you find the best patterns, in dry or wet mud?

54. What sort of things will sink deepest into wet soil? Provide objects of the same mass but with different-sized surface areas, to give experience of pressure being a combination of force and area. For example, the three different faces of a normal brick could be used.

55. If you find any animals' footprints in mud or damp sand you may like to make plaster casts of them.

You will need a strip of cartridge paper and some paper clips.

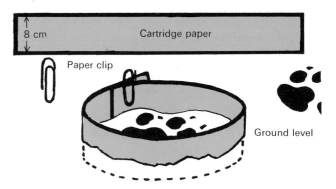

Place the paper round the footprint and secure with a paper clip.

Stir enough dental plaster of Paris into the water to fill the mould. The mixture should flow easily.

Pour into mould.

Continue other investigations while plaster sets.

Collect the cast and gently scrub away mud next day with an old toothbrush.

Label with the name of the animal, the date and the place where it was made.

A track on the beach. What made this footprint in the sand?

56. What parts of plants are hidden below the ground?

57. Shall we hunt for animals in the soil today?

Spread some earth or leaf litter on a piece of white rubber sheeting and gently sort through it. Hunting can be done at different depths. (See Volume 2 Part I.)

Using the other senses

Touching and feeling
Here experiences can be of different types.

Feeling surfaces and shapes
1. Shall we collect words that describe all the different things we can manage to feel in the playground, or along the path through the woods, on our waste ground, etc?

2. Let's make a chart to show how we can sort out our things by feeling.

Sorting by feeling						
Rough	**Smooth**	**Sharp**	**Blunt**	**Warm**	**Cold**	**Sticky**
Bark of the oak tree	Pebbles	Thorn Edge of the flint			Iron rail-ings	Horse-chest-nut buds

3. Shall we see whether things feel the same if we use different parts of ourselves? Try using:

Tips of right and left fingers.
Middle of forearm.
Elbow.
Back of neck (with help of partner).
Big toe.
Heel, etc.

4. Is there any part of you that cannot feel?

5. I wonder what it would be like to feel the same thing with a hot and then a cold hand. Could you suggest any way in which we could do this?

6. Descriptive writing about tactile experiences can be encouraged, for example about:

Jumping into the swimming pool.
Feeling snow.
Damp bulb fibre.
The barks of trees.
The petals of a rose.

7. Is it really colder in the shade than in the sun? How could you check whether your feelings are right or wrong?

Why does it feel warmer under the porch than in the the middle of the playground?

8. Here is a game: with each hand in turn feel ten things your friend finds for you in the school grounds. How many can you name without looking?

9. I wonder who can find their way round the edge of the playground by feeling and not looking.

10. What can you find out about the way blind people manage to find their way out of doors?

11. Look for damage caused by trampling—other things can be injured when your feet touch them.

Feeling the effects of forces
1. What can you feel against your faces today but cannot see? Choose a windy day for this.

2. If you stand facing in different directions does the feeling alter?

3. Hold up a wet finger.

Can you feel anything?

4. Where is the wind coming from today?

5. Where is the wind blowing towards?

Link with compass directions if appropriate.

6. What does the weather vane tell us about the wind?

7. How would you know the wind was blowing if you couldn't feel? (By seeing plants moving, paper blown along, washing on the line fluttering, etc.)

8. Do the clouds move in the same direction as the wind?

9. What makes that hawthorn bush such a queer shape?

10. Do you find the wind blowing harder on one day than another? You could estimate this by feeling, but what could you do to check this more accurately?

Feeling the resistance
to the air

11. Is it possible to describe the difference in the feel of still and rushing water?

12. If you find a lot of things that seem to be the same size is it possible to arrange them in order (heaviest first) by feeling? Do you know how to check your ideas about this by using the amount a rubber band stretches? (See page 55, no. 12a.)

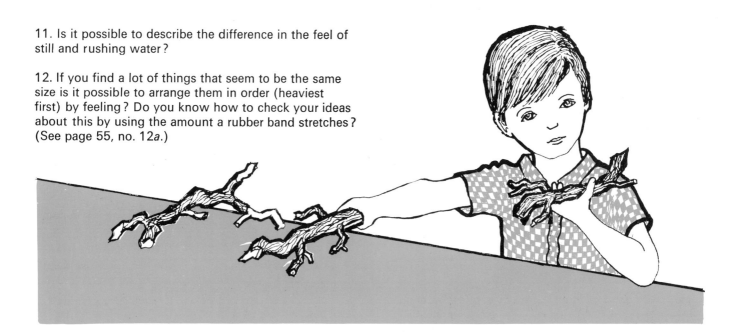

13. Do heavy things fall to the ground quicker than light things?

14. Which dogs pull hardest when you take them for walks on leads?

Measure the increase in length of very strong rubber bands attached to the dogs' leads. The bands can be made from the inner tubes of car tyres.

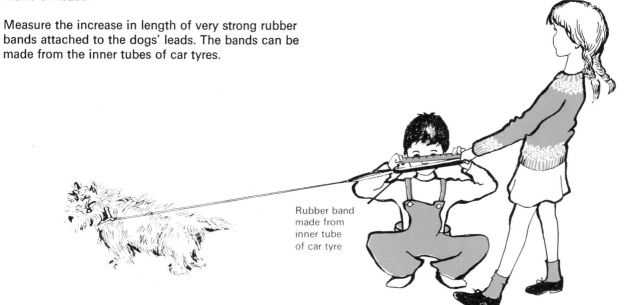

Rubber band made from inner tube of car tyre

Listening

1. If we go to different places in the school grounds I wonder whether we shall hear the same or different sounds.

2. I wonder who can find the most interesting way of making a sound out of doors.

3. We could try to collect high and low sounds.

4. What sort of sounds are easiest to hear over long distances? I wonder whether anybody could think of a way of trying to find out.

5. Are we all equally good at hearing? What could we do to test ourselves? (Tests can be designed by means of discussion.)

Words about sounds	Listening around our school			Words about sounds
	Near the gate	By the swimming pool	In the middle of the field	
Roaring . Tapping . Clattering . Rustling . . Sighing .	Mrs Brown walking Lorry Ambulance siren	Children shouting and splashing	Skylark singing as it rises Bee buzzing Wind blowing	Screaming . Rumbling . Cracking . Whistling . . Swishing

Children can stand at equal distances from the teacher, and then walk away until sounds made by her, such as ringing a bell, are inaudible. The distances achieved can then be measured.

6. Is one test like this enough for you to be sure about yourselves?

7. How many times do you think you should re-test yourselves?

8. Should the teacher make the same or different sounds for each re-test?

9. How do you know whether an aeroplane is approaching or disappearing if you cannot see it?

10. Is there any difference between the sounds of motors and lorries driving up and down hills?

11. It might be a good idea to try to set up a string telephone or speaking tube so that we could send messages across the field without shouting.

12. Which is the quickest way of getting a message across the field—signalling, shouting, or using the speaking tube? Use a length of garden hose pipe as a speaking tube.

13. In what sort of places can you find echoes?

14. Here is an out-of-school activity: collecting words about sounds in different places and making an interesting vocabulary book, for example about:

Traffic on the motorway.
Early morning on the farm.
A stormy night.
A hot summer afternoon.

Is he getting the message?

15. Here is a poem* that could be read to children by the teacher, to stimulate interest in listening and to inspire them to try and share their experiences through writing.

I like noise.
The whoop of a boy, the thud of a hoof
The rattle of rain on a galvanised roof,
The hubbub of traffic, the roar of a train,
The throb of machinery numbing the brain,
The switching of wires in an overhead tram,
The rush of the wind, a door on the slam,
The boom of thunder, the crash of the waves,
The din of a river that races and raves,
The crack of a rifle, the clank of a pail,
The strident tattoo of a swift-slapping sail—
From any old sound that the silence destroys
Arises a gamut of soul stirring joys
I like noise.

Smelling

1. Who can find something outside the classroom with a strong smell, for example:

Smoke from the bonfire.
The field after the gang mower has been at work.
The lavender border.
The manure heap.
Near the canteen.
The petrol station.
The fish shop?

2. When you have discovered a smell, can you find out how far you can get from it before you stop smelling it?

Is this distance you move from the smell the same in every direction?

What do you think causes the differences?

Which way is the wind blowing today?

3. Shall we make a collection of things with different smells for the Discovery Table? It would be a good idea to make a word list to go with them.

*'Noise' by J. Pope. *Words Take Wings*, A Time for Poetry, *Book 2, E. J. Arnold and Sons Ltd.*

What about another collection of things which have no smells?

4. Here is a game. Two or three children should go out of the room. Scent is then released into the air with a spray. The children enter and try to locate the point of release by smelling.

5. Do flowers with smells have more insect visitors than those with no smell? Count the visitors to selected plants in a border.

Tasting

This should be avoided out of doors. If in out-of-school time children attempt to repeat activities encouraged by teachers they may run the risk of eating *poisonous things*.

Even non-poisonous fruits and leaves may be covered with toxic sprays or dust.

Work in school concerned with investigating tastes of sweets and cooking is appropriate. Following recipes is an excellent way of introducing children to ideas involved in weighing. (See page 55, no. 12.)

Making collections

Although this activity should be based as far as possible on children's own suggestions, the teacher can introduce the idea of *conservation* in relation to a meaningful situation by:

a. Offering a choice of suggestions to children with few ideas so that different individuals are encouraged to look for different things.

b. Making sensible arrangements beforehand to avoid unnecessary duplication of specimens, ie one specimen per group rather than one specimen per child.

c. Letting children know of any rarities in the collecting area that should *not* be touched or trampled upon.

Ideas for collections (sets)
1. Common wild flowers of the month.

2. Garden flowers of the month.

3. Grasses (June).

4. Tree flowers that come before leaves (early spring).

5. Tree flowers that come after leaves (late spring and summer).

6. Evergreens (winter—December).

7. Twigs of deciduous trees (January, February).

8. Leaves:

a. For shape (summer).
b. For colour (autumn).

What is interesting about these two sets of leaves?

9. Paintings of fungi (autumn). Warning about poisonous plants should be given.

10. Seaweeds.

11. Mosses.

12. General collection of non-flowering plants.

13. Seeds and fruits.

14. Things that damage and alter plants (galls, fungi, leaf miners, leaf feeders, etc).

15. Protective devices in plants and animals (thorns, hairs, stings, poison, thick cuticle, camouflage, etc).

16. Plants with interesting smells, e.g. herbs.

17. Animal tracks providing clues about:

a. Movement:
Footprints (see page 20 for directions for making casts).

b. Feeding:
Holes in nuts.
Nuts split in halves.
Cones eaten by squirrels and crossbills.
Damaged bark due to rabbits, deer, etc.
Bird pellets.
Droppings (handle wearing rubber gloves).

c. Body coverings:
Wool (sheep).
Fur (rabbit).
Hairs (badger, squirrel, fox).
Feathers (birds).
Cast skins (reptiles, insects, crustaceans).
Shells (molluscs).

d. Models of home-making—holes made by:
Sand martins.
Ants.
Mice and voles.
Badgers.
Foxes.
Woodpeckers.

Droppings, hairs and footprints nearby or size or position, can provide clues about the makers of the holes.

e. Body structure and size:
Empty chrysalid cases.
Skulls.
Bones.

Sorting a collection of bones

18. Objects to illustrate different tints and tones of one colour (useful in building up concepts of colours).

19. Different things that can be described by one adjective, eg round things.

In one school, a child's collection consisted of a drawing-pin head, fruit from a plane tree, a drawing of a hole in the ground, a pebble, a drawing of a puddle, a section across a cut tree trunk, the opening of a waste-paper basket.

'But nature does not provide identical objects . . . The action of putting things which are not identical into a group or class is so familiar that we forget how sweeping it is.'* This process depends on recognising things in a collection to be alike when they are not identical.

*Bronowski, J., The Common Sense of Science, Penguin, 1968.

Further suggestions for collections that illustrate conceptual ideas:

Exciting things.
Delicate things.
Menacing things.
Mysterious things.

20. Interesting shapes (two- and three-dimensional).

21. Patterns and shapes giving experience of:

a. Bilateral and radial symmetry; asymmetry (see pages 61 and 62, no. 4).

b. Use of units in repetition, reversal, alternation, rotation and superimposed upon one another (see page 64, no. 7).

c. Patterns not involving units—interesting for their beauty.

Wing patterns

22. Rocks, stones and pebbles.

23. Materials used in building a house.

24. Materials used as top dressings for roads.

Are they different in different parts of the country?
Do they correspond to the rocks of the area?
Which ones are mixed with tar?

25. Fossils.

26. Soils.

27. Flavours from the supermarket.

How many does mother use?

28. Very unusual things.

29. Things more than fifty years old.

30. A collection of pictures made with a camera.

Using collections
Collections are only worth making when children can
be encouraged to use them for further investigation and
comparison on returning to the classroom after outdoor
expeditions.

Suggestions for comparative studies
1. Colours of flowers: finding the most commonly
occurring colour in flowers collected each month.

2. The number and arrangement of petals in different
flowers.

3. The length of time different flowers remain in bloom—
this may affect a plant's chances of becoming pollinated
(see page 56).

4. Leaves:

Shape.
Size (length, width, area).
Type of edge.
Subdivision into parts or leaflets.

5. Autumn leaves. A chart can be made to show:

The dates of colour changes.
The colours to which leaves change.
The date of fall from the tree.
The shape of the scar remaining on the twig.

6. Twigs in winter. A winter recognition chart for a
collection of twigs of deciduous trees can be constructed.

| Name of tree | Buds | | | | Arrangement on twig | Colour of bark | Leaf scars |
| | Colour | Shape | Size | | | | |
			Length	Width			
Ash	Black	Short, broad at base				Green-ish-grey	
Elm							
Birch							
Beech							
Horse-chestnut							
Sweet chestnut							
Oak							
Lime							
Sycamore							
Willow							

7. A diary about a collection of twigs showing differences in their rates of development from the time of enlargement and opening of their buds.

8. Attachments to fruits and seeds.

Observing the different effects of retaining and removing plumes, wings, etc, before allowing fruits to fall.

9. Birds' feathers: their colour, and their shape and size in relation to position on the body.

Making a collage with feathers

10. Pebbles: colour, shape, size, mass (see pages 74 and 75).

11. Rocks: colour, mass, position on scale of hardness, effects of water, effects of weak acid.

12. Colours: the effect of the same colour against different backgrounds; different colours against the same background; the visibility of different colours.

By making use of these ideas for studying collections over and over again in different places and carefully observing the results, children can develop good ways of comparing the different places they explore.

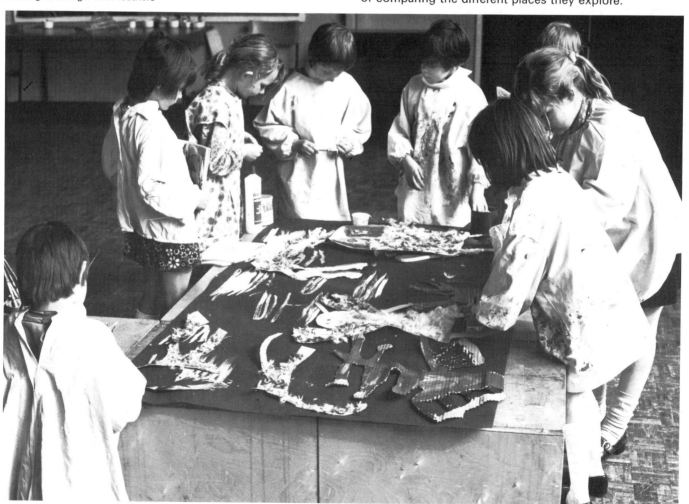

Some six- to seven-year-olds chose many interesting colours and textures to fill in the outlines of these birds

Sorting and arranging collections

Much sorting and grouping should be part of children's comparative studies. They will often find that a good way of recording comparisons and their decisions about sorting is by some concrete arrangement of specimens. Therefore much of the classroom activity following an outdoor expedition may well revolve around the Nature (Discovery, Investigation) Table or Corner. This is the place where ideas about sets (pages 39 and 40, nos. 3 and 4) can be argued and much discovered through trial and error about size, spacing and effective colours. The need for some explanatory headings will give good reasons for learning and writing new words and the wish to replace or add to displays can initiate further outdoor exploration. But there have been many times when these possibilities have not been appreciated and the Nature Table has become a classroom 'dump' which everybody ignores. It is more likely to arouse continuous interest if the teacher gives careful thought to ways in which many children can become involved in using it.

In the first place, the children must have surfaces on which they can set out their finds and records. Horizontal space can be provided in any part of the room if low mobile storage units with flat tops are available. In small rooms where these would occupy too much space, vertical spaces can be provided by areas of perforated board fixed to the walls of classrooms and corridors or used in the construction of portable screens. In old buildings it is often possible to find interesting alcoves that serve as ideal sites for small displays. These areas together with a generous supply of containers, small trays and peg-board fittings give children the facilities they need for varying ways in which they can group and set out their materials and specimens.

If children are encouraged to assume full responsibility for displays relating to their outdoor work, they will soon cooperate in devising different arrangements.

At this stage their teachers can encourage them to be critical of each other's efforts and this is what leads to active thinking and lively argument.

It is essential that areas for display and investigation should be regarded as dynamic parts of the school environment. There should be frequent change of theme and this can be achieved without difficulty if all children become convinced through their teacher's interest and appreciation that their ideas and efforts are welcome.

It is also necessary to evolve some kind of rota system for the day-to-day maintenance of these displays especially when they include living material. Not only does this ensure the sharing of chores, it is also a good way of encouraging the children who are not the original thinkers to participate in the follow-up to outdoor activities.

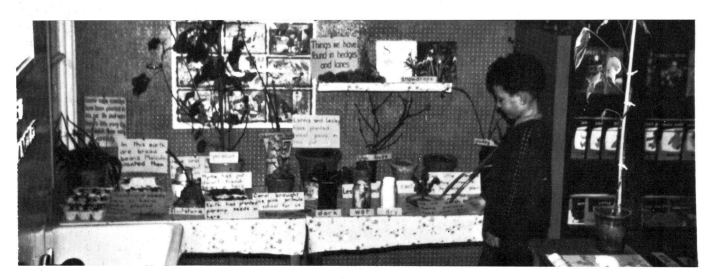

3 Observing numerical and spatial aspects of the environment

Now it is time to consider some of the investigations children can be encouraged to make and talk about as their interest in quantity, size and position of the things around them develops.

At the same time, it is useful to know what conceptual ideas, of a numerical and spatial nature, these investigations might bring within children's experience. So these, too, have been set out in this chapter.

Although conceptual ideas will only form and deepen very slowly in children's minds, owing to their abstract nature, it is not too soon for teachers to regard the understanding of such ideas as long-term objectives to which their present work with children might contribute.

In what follows, however, clear distinctions have been made between concepts and the essentially concrete experiences through which they may begin to be formed. This has been done in the text by printing each concept in colour and following it immediately with suggestions for conversations and activities in which young children could become involved.

Dealing with discrete quantities, that is, separate things that can be counted

1

Concept: one thing associated with another— early ideas of relationships

Here's a deserted nest. Let's see what the bird used in making it.

The nest is made of twigs, grass and moss.

Note the twig across the nest to hold it securely

Other examples
I wonder what left these droppings. Rabbits ⟷ droppings.

make
Spiders ⟷ webs.

blows from
Pollen ⟷ catkins.

stop us touching
Stings ⟷ nettles.

is just like
The stick caterpillar ⟷ this twig.

have   on their
Ladybirds ⟷ spots ⟷ wing cases.

2
Concept: the idea of sets
Making collections. See pages 28-32 for suggestions.

Vocabulary
Set, collection, class, belongs with, goes together.

3
Concept: recognition of 'things in a set to be
alike when they are not identical'*
Comparing and sorting finds after returning from outdoor
expeditions. If we put PE hoops side by side
on the Nature Table, can you place things that you
think should go together inside each one of them?

*Bronowski, J., The Common Sense of Science,
Penguin, 1968, page 27.

Concept: partition of sets into sub-sets
Now can you think of ways of dividing the things in
each hoop into smaller and smaller collections?

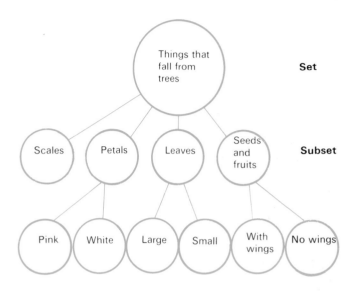

Concept: intersecting sets
How can we arrange the hoop containing round things
and the hoop with brown things to show that some of
our finds belong inside both hoops?

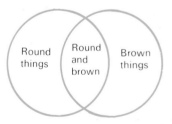

Concept: disjoint sets—no members in common
Now can you find some collections of things that are
quite different from each other?

Vocabulary
Alike, unlike, similar, different, belong, go together.

4

Look at all the birds on the lake. Which ones could be put in a little set together because they are alike?

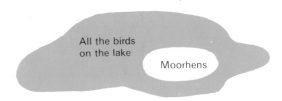

Other examples

5

a. I wonder how many things will pass our school during playtime today?

Counters of different colours can be matched to different things observed and a chart constructed.

Cars	Lorries	Men	Dogs

b. Travelling by bus to a study area:

One child can be matched to each seat.
Each child needs one ticket.

c. Arranging displays of wild flowers in the classroom:

One bottle is required for each flower.
One label is needed for each bottle.

Vocabulary
The same as, too many, not enough, too few, more than, less than.

6

When is the road outside our school busiest?

Pairs of children can take quarter-hour watches.
Each vehicle passing may be represented by a stroke.

Time	Vehicles Passing	Frequency
9.00–9.15	LHT LHT LHT III	18
9.15–9.30	LHT II	7
9.30–9.45	LHT LHT	10
9.45–10.00	LHT III	8
10.00–10.15	LHT IIII	9

Another inquiry might consist of counting how many birds visit the bird table, and how often they come.

7

I wonder why all those cows are waiting by the gate.

Who milks them? One milker ⟷ many cows.

Who can find the flower with the most petals?

How many children can use the swimming pool at one time?

Many flowers ⟷ one meadow

Many acorns ⟷ one tree

One hive ⟷ many bees

Many water fleas ⟷ one pond

Many wood ants ⟷ one ant hill

One nest ⟷ several eggs

Many pebbles ⟷ one beach

One bull ⟷ many cows

8
Concept: association of many to many
Discussion topics
Many barnacles and limpets on all the rocks.
Many plants in all the flower beds in the park.
Many leaves on all the trees in the wood.
Many grains of wheat on all the ears of corn.

9
Concept: cardinal numbers 1-9
Now we know that two things alike make a pair, it
would be a good idea to collect things in twos, or we
could say pairs.

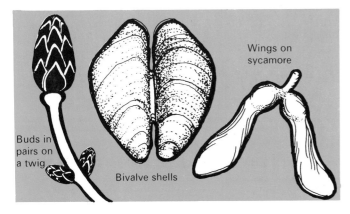

Wings on sycamore

Buds in pairs on a twig

Bivalve shells

Similar treatment for other numbers
This cuckoo flower has four petals. How many more
flowers with that number of petals can you find for our
Discovery Table?

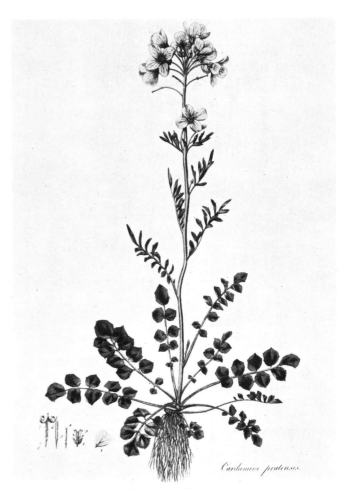

Cuckoo flower (*Cardamine pratensis*)

A wood might be a good place to hunt for leaves
divided into leaflets (threes, fives, sevens).

Concept: use of symbols to represent the total
number of things in a set
Can you use some of the things you found while we
were in the wood to make up sets that match the
numbers on these boxes? When you have a set in each
box, put them on the Nature Table.

10

How many materials did you find while beachcombing?

How many seeds do vetch pods from the waste ground hold?

I wonder how many different grasses we could manage to collect this week.

11

A wild flower must not be collected unless more than ten of the same kind can be left growing. This is a rule for looking after the countryside that we must learn before going out.

If you collect two bags of leaf litter from different places in the wood, we could see whether one lot contains more or fewer small animals than the other.

Let us see whether there are more pieces of wood than plastic or metal things in the material we found while we were beachcombing.

Looking for records:

The pod with the most seeds.
The animal with the most legs.
The flower with the least number of petals.
The tendril with the most turns.
The ladybird with the least number of spots.

Vocabulary
Many, few, a lot, hardly any, common, rare, plentiful, scarce.

12

Discussion topics
The number of things involved when:

a. The same number of seeds are planted close together or further apart in the school garden.

b. The spacing of the pebbles on the Nature Table is altered.

13

How many seagulls can you count following behind the plough?

Keep very still and watch. You may be able to count the number of times the blackbird brings food to its young in a quarter of an hour.

How many plants did you take from that row of radishes when you thinned it out?

It would be interesting to choose one plant and find out how many seeds it has produced.

Human pulse beats or the heart beats of the school rabbit can also be counted.

14

Concept: ordinal numbers—symbols representing position of things in ordered sequences
On which step does your 'Slinky' spring come to rest most frequently?

Get yourselves in order of height with the smallest first.

If you number the caterpillars in the order in which they turn into chrysalids, we can then make a guess at the order in which we can expect them to become butterflies.

Record 1st, 2nd, . . . days of the month on weather charts, nature calendars, etc.

15

Concept: addition—bringing together two or more small sets of things to make a larger set
a. Recording results of birdwatching for ten minutes each day after scattering food on the lawn.

	Black-birds	Star-lings	Spar-rows	Robins	All the birds seen
Monday	2	4	3		9
Tuesday	1	2	4	1	8
Wednesday	1	5	6	2	14
Thursday		3	4		7
Friday	2	3	5	1	11

b. Brightening a corner of the playground:

If we plant our bulbs at different depths in a tub, it will hold 10 crocuses, 3 hyacinths, 3 tulips. How many bulbs will that be altogether?

c. How many peas have we grown from one seed? (A test from the school vegetable plot.)

Pick all the pods off a plant. Open each pod and put the set of peas you find inside in a basin.

When you have finished, you can find out how many peas were on that plant.

d. Here is a game to be played with pebbles on the beach.

A number is called by the teacher; children try to find two sets of pebbles that can be put together to make the set the number called represents.

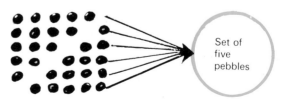

Set of five pebbles

Concept: the commutative law of addition
Discussion topic
Is there any difference between putting together 4 and 1 or 1 and 4 pebbles?

16

Concept: subtraction—finding the number of things required to make a smaller set of things up to a larger set

On which half of the lawn can you find the most dandelions?

Can you discover how many more are on one side?

After dividing the lawn by pegging down a rope, the flower heads or beads representing the flowers from the two areas are matched and the number of flowers or beads required to make the smaller set up to the larger set can be noted.

Matching beads to daisies

The same method can be used for comparing:

Quantities of daisies or white clover flowers on areas of lawn.
Weeds on trampled and untrampled lengths of path.
Groundsel seedlings on tended and neglected flower beds.

Concept: subtraction—noting the number of things remaining after a small set of things has been removed from a larger set

How many of the six acorns you planted three weeks ago have no roots showing yet?

Matching beads representing daisies in different hoops

Shall we try to discover something about the bluetits that can eat peanuts from a string?

Thread twenty peanuts together and hang them from the hook on the bird table on coming to school. Then fill in on a chart the number left at the end of the day. If you do that regularly each day we could discover whether the tits eat the same or different amounts of nuts each day at different times.

There were twelve flowerpots on a pile, but I believe the frost has cracked some. Could you find out how many are still fit to use?

17

Concept: multiplication or repeated addition

If you want to find out when the car park across the road holds the most cars, they will have to be counted every quarter of an hour. It might be easier for the children to count in twos.

I wonder how many wheels all the cars that pass the school gate during playtime have. If you drop a counter in a box for every car you see, that should give you the number of fours you will need to come to all those wheels.

Discussion topic

The number of plants altogether when they are set out in regular rows, eg:

Tulips in a park flower bed.
Conifer seedlings in a forestry seed bed.
Cabbages on an allotment.

Concept: commutative law of multiplication

When you look at the plants from one end you can see more rows than when you stand at the side. See whether this makes any difference to the number of all the plants on the bench.

Three fives or five threes?

18

Concept: division as repeated subtraction

All the eggs our hens have laid in a week are in the basket. How many people from the over-sixties club will be able to have two each?

John's father has given us a box of African marigolds. How many of you can get three plants for your plots out of it?

Concept: division as partitioning

We shall need a collection of conkers in three equal-sized sets for the hardness trials. Who would like to arrange that for us?

19

Concept: fractions—parts of whole things

Discussion topics

Arrangements by which whole things are divided into parts. Here are some examples·

Leaves by midribs.
Segmented bodies of caterpillars.
Head, thorax and abdomen of insects.

Dealing with continuous quantities, that is, things that can be measured

1

Concept: similarity and difference with regard to size

Here are some ways in which sizes may be compared:

a. On the waste ground:

Let us see how many different plants we can find that are taller than a ragwort plant.

Now let us make a collection of plants smaller than a ragwort. When we get back to school I should like you to arrange all the plants on the Nature Table with the shortest ones in front and the taller ones behind.

b. I wonder whether groundsel plants alter very much as they grow. If you collect all the seedlings you can find and arrange them in order of size; you might be able to find out more about that.

Shepherd's purse, willowherb, limpet shells, would also be suitable for arranging in order of size.

c. Looking for records:

The shortest leaf, the narrowest leaf, the biggest weed, the thinnest stem, the thickest twig, the smallest animal, the longest root, the largest stone, the longest piece of seaweed, the daisy with the longest stalk, the tallest goose grass plant in the hedgerow.

d. Finding things that are of a suitable size to:

Be stored in the garage.
Use the nesting box.
Pass under the bridge.
See over the fence.
Travel back to school in the collecting box.
Reach the lowest branch.

Vocabulary
Bigger, larger, longer, wider, thicker, smaller, shorter, narrower, too big, too small, not big enough, not small enough, the same size as, largest, smallest.

2
Concept: the relative nature of size
I wonder who can be observant enough to find some of these things for the Discovery Table:

Big acorn.
Big lemon.
Large flower.
Large owl pellet.
Long catkin.
Large shell.
Short banana.
Small bottle.
Short twig.
Narrow piece of tubing.
Small deserted bird's nest.
Plant with a thin stem.
Small orange.

Now can you sort the things you have found so that the larger ones are on one side of the table and the smaller ones on the other side?

The drawing above was done by a six-year-old child after a visit to The Natural History Museum in London. The way this child has drawn children in relation to the dinosaur shows how he has developed a good idea of relative size.

Discussion topics
Something we began by calling big may seem quite small when we match it against something unlike itself.

We need to be able to measure things to tell people what they are really like.

3

What can we use for finding out how big or small things are?

Could we see how many times a stretched-out hand (hand span) could fit against a window-sill?

What other parts of ourselves could we put against things? First finger, forearm, a foot length, own height.

Our hand spans are different

A six-year-old with his model made from scrap material. His ideas about size and proportion are developing well

How many hand spans?

48

4
Concept: beginning of estimation

If Roger lies down, how many times do you think he would fit along the side of the flower bed?

Using Roger as the unit for estimating the length of the lawn

How many 'Rogers' do you think would be:

As tall as the wall, the lamp post?
As long as the path?

5

Concept: use of arbitrary units for measuring distances

John and Ruth have both measured with hand spans the height of the hollyhock as it has grown.

Why have they got different answers? (Children vary in size.)

Discussion topics
We need something that is always the same size to match against things we want to measure. Here are some examples:

Matchbox lengths against bricks, growing plants, leaves; wooden laths against farm gates, stiles, railings, edges of lawns; lengths of string round tree stumps, circular bird baths.

Using a matchbox as a unit of length

What can we do with the piece that nearly always gets left over when we measure with these things?

Concept: measuring devices giving better approximations

Discussion topics
We need measures divided into smaller parts to fit against the pieces left over. The following could be introduced:

Metre sticks divided into centimetres and 10-centimetre lengths.
Tape measures marked in centimetres.
Ropes marked in metres.
A 'click wheel' with circumference of 1 metre.

Measuring in standard units of length

6

At this stage children should be encouraged to revisit sites of their earlier explorations to make use of their increased skill in measuring distances. Much more precise detail can be added to earlier findings and comparisons.

Records of changes in plants and animals under observation in the school grounds and classroom should become more exact and therefore more significant.

Finding distances all the way round:

a. The edges of round things: wheels, cut surfaces of tree stumps, garden tubs.

b. Other shapes: lawns, patch of waste ground, flower beds in the park, a field, pathways.

Concepts: diagonal; diameter; radius

Children can be encouraged to measure many objects providing experience of these concepts.

Examples

The strengthening bar on a farm gate.

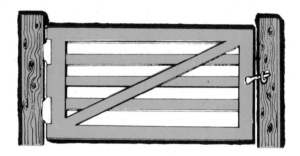

Road signs.

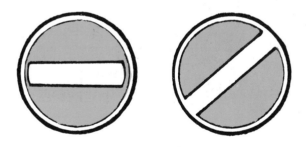

Letter N in signs and advertisements.

The spokes of wheels.

Concept: error

Estimations should also be attempted by matching (in imagination) the height or length of something of known size against an object. The extent of error in the estimation can then be found by further measurement.

Knowledge gained from measuring and estimating should be reflected in the children's conversation, and in any charts or other written records it may be appropriate for them to make.

	Estimated distance	Measured distance	Difference error
Height of bird table	1m 25cm	1m 40cm	15 cm
Height of hogweed	2 m	2 m 7 cm	7 cm
Across rock pool	5 m	4 m 50 cm	50 cm

7

What seems to happen to:

Lamp posts farther and farther along the street?
The electricity pylons in a row?
The telegraph posts along the road?
The trawler as it leaves harbour and moves out to sea?
The skylark as it flies upward and downward singing all the time?
The aeroplane as it moves across the sky?
Furrows across a field?

Shall we walk on to the next pylon (or lamp post) and have a closer look at it?

Here are some comparisons to make:

Chimney pots on houses and on the ground in the builder's yard.
TV aerials on chimney pots and on the ground.
Aeroplanes in the air and on the ground at the airport (during a visit).

What do you think people and buildings on the ground would look like if you could watch them from:

The Post Office Tower?
The Stone Gallery of St Paul's Cathedral?
Up in an aeroplane?

Now let's look at each other standing in different places on the school field.

Are they really becoming smaller?

What other things could we find to measure in different positions:

A cricket stump upright and lying on the ground?
Parts of a gate shut and open?
Have they altered in size?

Concept: early ideas of reduction for drawing to scale
Provide groups of children with empty picture frames and encourage them to hold them up and look at different outdoor views enclosed by the frames.

Discussion topic
Could the objects enclosed really fit within the dimensions of the frames?

8

Concept: area—all over a surface

It might be interesting to try to make a list of all the things you can find that spread over the ground or other flat surfaces:

Grass seed, Lawn Plus, moss killer, spread over the lawn.
Creeping buttercup, white clover, moss, spreading over bare ground.
Tar and top dressing all over the road surface.
Concrete over the path.
Asphalt all over the playground.
Roofing felt over the roof of a chicken house.

Concept: measurement of size of surfaces in arbitrary units

How can we find out whether all the patios outside the classrooms of our school are the same size? (By counting the slabs covering them.)

Can you find any other surfaces about which we can find out more, by counting the things of which they consist?

	made with	
Walls	⟶	bricks.

	laid from	
Lawns	⟶	turfs.

	covered by	
Roofs	⟶	tiles.

	covered by	
The surface of water in a jam jar	⟶	plants

of duckweed.

	look as if they consist of	
If you draw some leaves in outline on graph paper, they might	⟶	squares. We

could count them. (Ignore less than half squares.)

Spreading top dressing over the road surface

9

Concepts: fluidity; solidity

a. We may find some interesting things today during our nature walk. What should we use for carrying them home?
For solid things: tins, plastic bags, if damp; haversacks, pockets, hands, if dry.
For liquid things: non-porous plastic containers (avoid glass).

b. Try to find out more about the behaviour of things on flat surfaces. How many things can you find that rock, wobble or remain quite still, when you put them down?

What happens if the milkman has an accident and drops a bottle of milk? (Rapid spread of liquid. Make good use of spills in the classroom.)

We could watch the workmen tarring the road. (Slow spread of liquid.)

Shall we try to find some more people dealing with liquid things? Here are some of the activities we might look at:

Distributing petrol at the garage.
Filling the oil tank of a central heating system.
Milking cows.
Delivering milk.
Filling and emptying a canal lock.

Collect news of events involving liquids: floods, cloud bursts, volcanic eruptions.

Discussion topics
Liquids spread and run away unless they are put in something. They turn into the shape of whatever contains them (pipes, tanks, bottles, etc).

How many shapes can you make a liquid take?

Vocabulary
Solid, liquid, run, spread, fluid, viscous, pour, flow.

10
Concept: volumes of liquids
As they make field observations about liquids children should be extending their experience through work with water in the classroom, such as siphoning, and by comparing different amounts various containers hold.

First measures will be simple vessels in common usage, eg bottles, cups, baby's feeding bottle.

Experience of measuring in arbitrary units such as cupfuls will eventually lead to a need for standard measures for capacity (litre, $\frac{1}{2}$ litre).

Concept: conservation of volume
The alteration of the shape of the same liquid when put in different containers can be recorded; and there can be discussion on whether the amount is the same or different when its shape alters.

11
Concept: comparison of sizes (volumes) of solid things
What happens when you put a stone in a jar of water? (The water level rises.)

We could measure the distance the water moves upwards for different stones.

How much water does Peter's stone push up?

Discussion topics

Peter's stone pushed up most water. It must have been the biggest stone because the water moved up the greatest amount to make room for it.

Later, when children have become accustomed to measuring capacity, they can catch the amount of water displaced and measure it.

Stones	Rise of water
John's stone	2 cm
Mary's stone	3 cm
Peter's stone	4 cm
Katherine's stone	3 cm
Martin's stone	2 cm

12

Concept: heaviness and lightness
For further suggestions on experience of the force of gravity acting on things of different size, see page 24, nos. 12 and 13.

When two things feel similar, how can we decide which is heavier?

a. By seeing which object suspended from a rubber band causes the greatest amount of stretching.

b. By comparing them on a balance.

c. By balancing each object against washers (arbitrary units of measurement).

How many washers will balance with the stone?

Vocabulary

Heavier, lighter, different, the same as, big, small.

55

13

Concept: units of time

Shall we try to make a list of all the things we can find happening regularly?

The tick of a clock.
Our own pulse-beats.
The click of the trundle wheel.
The beat of a cement mixer.
The throb of a pump.
The movement of a seesaw up and down.
High and low tide.
Night and day.
Spring, summer, autumn, winter.

When children appear to be ready, the teacher can help them to find a way of measuring a length of time by counting the number of times something happens regularly, eg a pendulum swinging.

See Volume 2 Part 2, for suggestions for making a simple timing device.

Concept: different intervals of time

Can you find out how long you take:

To get to school?
To feed the gerbils?
To weed your garden plot?
To travel by bus to the woods?
To watch sand run through an egg timer?

Starting and finishing times to be noted. Clocks and seconds timers will be required.

Concept: passing time

Regularly record the time taken for changes in growth and development to occur, for instance:

The growth of seedlings in and out of doors.
The growth of plants under different environmental conditions.
Changes during the metamorphosis of frogs, butterflies, etc.
The growth of pets.

Shall we try to discover which wild flower by the hedge

	Our tadpole diary	
march 20th	We put some frog spawn into our tank	
21st	they have grown one has come out	
22nd	two with long tails the others are big	
26th	they all have long tails and move about	
April 5th	We can see their mouths they are growing bigger	
26th	they are big and have more shape	
may 4th	one has 2 back legs	
11th	more tadpoles have 2 back legs	
15th	one has his front legs	
22nd	some are frogs losing their tails	
	then we let the frogs go free	

Hedgerow flowers	Days in bloom
	1 2 3 4 5 6 7 8 9 10 11 12 13 14 15
Hedge woundwort	√ √ √ √ √ √
Cuckoo pint	√ √ √ √ √ √ √ √ √ √ √
Hedge parsley	√ √ √ √ √ √ √
Stitchwort	√ √ √ √ √ √
Red campion	√ √ √ √ √
Stinging nettle	√ √ √ √ √ √ √ √ √ √ √ √ √ √ √

56

remains in bloom for the longest time? Tie red tape round the stems of the flowers which are under observation.

Concept: reference points of time (standard time)
At what time each day shall we:

Look at the sky for clouds? 09.00 hours.
Fill in the weather chart? 10.30 hours.
Make a count of the number of seagulls on the school field? 14.00 hours.
Mark the position of the shadow thrown by the shadow stick? 09.00, 10.00, 11.00 . . . hours.

Vocabulary
Quickly, slowly, soon, long ago, yesterday, tomorrow, past, now, present, future.

14
Concept: speed as distance covered in a given time

Measure a length of Marley guttering. Now find out how long it takes a snail to move along it. Use a seconds timer. What can you do to test whether the snail usually takes this amount of time to cover this distance? Repeat a number of times with the same snail to get an average. Does it seem to get tired and slow down?

Additional investigations
Find the time taken for:

Woodlice, caterpillars, etc, to travel along 1 m of Marley guttering.
Ping-pong balls to travel along 10 m of stream.
Matchsticks to travel along 10 m of the gutter after heavy rain.
Different children to swim the length of the school pool.

Find the member of the class who can:

Run a fixed distance (eg 50 m) in the shortest time.
Run the longest distance in a fixed time (2 minutes).

Compare the times that the same child takes to run the same distance:

Up and down a hill.
Along a winding route and a straight route.

Vocabulary
Slowly, quickly, rapid, fast, speed, rate.

From the Faber Story Book *edited by Kathleen Lines and illustrated by Alan Howard, published by Faber & Faber, 1961.*

Dealing with spatial experience

1

Concept: separation of common shapes from their surroundings

Making collections (to include pictures and drawings) of things that are:

Square	Circular
Rectangular	Semicircular
Cubic	Spherical
Triangular	Oval
Diamond-shaped	Cone-shaped
Hexagonal	Spirally curved

'I spy' games related to different shapes can be played during expeditions outside the school.

2

Concept: fitting shapes together—tessellation

Can you find some things that can fit together with no spaces between?

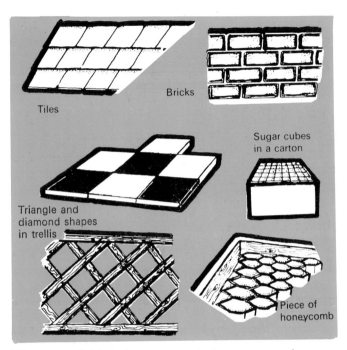

Tiles

Bricks

Triangle and diamond shapes in trellis

Sugar cubes in a carton

Piece of honeycomb

What sort of things have spaces between even when they are close together?

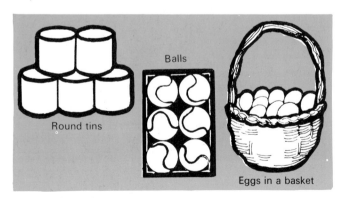

Round tins

Balls

Eggs in a basket

Discussion topic

Things with straight sides that fit together without spaces between, such as containers on lorries, and goods packed on the shelves of the supermarket.

Facets of the insect's compound eye fit together without spaces

Concept: amount of space between shapes

How can we find out how much space is not filled by pebbles in a jar?

Pour water into the jar until it just covers the pebbles, then carefully drain it into a measuring glass. Repeat several times and find the average.

If we fill the same jar with some of the pebbles mixed with smaller stones, and then with very small stones, can we fit more or less water into the jar the second time than we did the first time?

Concept: amount contained by different shapes

Which tins hold the most—round or square ones?

3

Concept: angles

If you look carefully you can find some different kinds of corners made when two lines meet. We call these different kinds of corners *angles*.

How many angles can you discover?

Concept: different kinds of angles

What sort of angles can be found most easily?
(Right angles.)

60

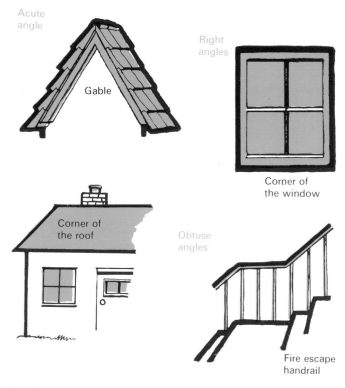

Acute angle

Gable

Right angles

Corner of the window

Corner of the roof

Obtuse angles

Fire escape handrail

Shall we make something for checking the shapes we think are right angles?

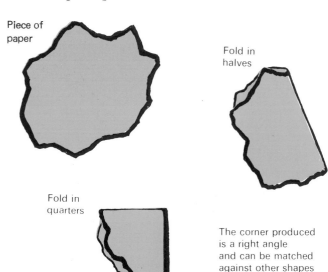

Piece of paper

Fold in halves

Fold in quarters

The corner produced is a right angle and can be matched against other shapes

4

How many things can you find that can be divided into two matching halves:

In many ways? (Radial symmetry.)

Primrose

Apple cut in halves

Wheel

Starfish

In how many ways can these things be cut into matching halves?

In only one way? (Bilateral symmetry.)

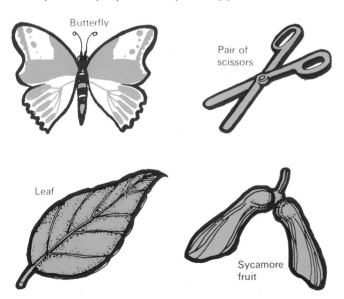

Butterfly

Pair of scissors

Leaf

Sycamore fruit

61

Can you find some things that cannot be divided into
two matching halves, eg a lump of rock, a castle?
See also page 31, no. 21*a*.

Vocabulary
Similar, unlike, alike, matching, equal, balance, the
same as.

5
Why can we see only part of the house? (It is behind,
half hidden by . . . .)

Where is the house in relation to the trees?

What prevents dogs getting into the garden? (A fence
all round.)

Where are the buds on the twig you have found?
(Alternate, opposite to each other.)

How many different arrangements of petals on flowers
can a group of children find? (Circular, opposite:
see Volume 2 Part 1.)

Choose a plant that is growing and find out the highest
and the lowest part of it.

If Mary, John and Jack stand in different places, can
you make up a drawing that shows where they are in
relation to each other?

Observe one child in relation to another on climbing
apparatus or adventure equipment.

High, higher and highest. Position of one child in relation to another
on the climbing apparatus

On a sunny day stand in different places and see what
happens to your shadow.

How can you get it in front of you? Does it remain the
same size when you move?

Vocabulary
Above, below, level with, opposite to, nearer, farther
away, higher than, lower than, to the right or left of,
through, between.

6

Concepts: verticality; horizontality; parallelism (always the same distance apart)

Some things stand upright, others are fixed in different positions. Shall we go out and see what we can discover about this?

Collect examples of things that are vertical, horizontal or parallel.

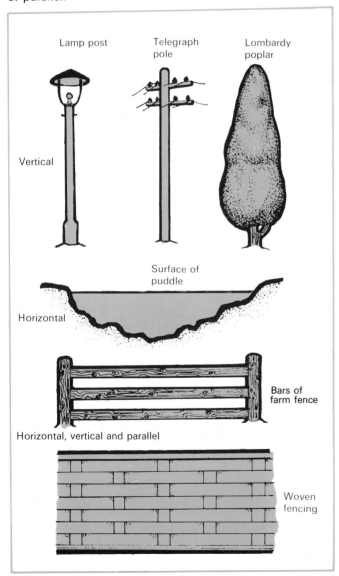

Lamp post   Telegraph pole   Lombardy poplar

Vertical

Surface of puddle

Horizontal

Bars of farm fence

Horizontal, vertical and parallel

Woven fencing

Shall we try to make some things for testing whether things are really horizontal or vertical?

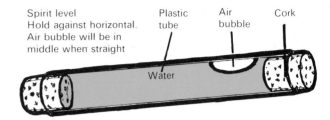

Spirit level
Hold against horizontal.
Air bubble will be in middle when straight

Plastic tube   Air bubble   Cork

Water

Is the pole vertical? Testing with a home-made plumb-line

63

7

Leaf printing is a good way of starting on this. Shall we see how many patterns we can make with our leaves by putting them in different positions before we print them?

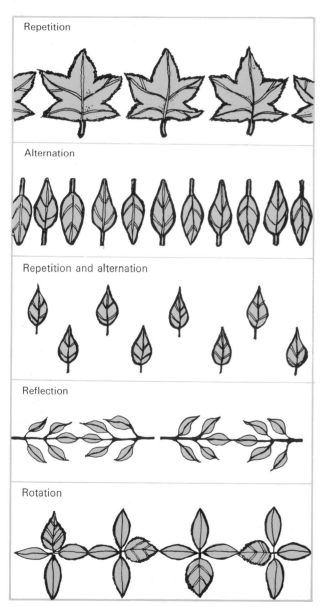

Repetition

Alternation

Repetition and alternation

Reflection

Rotation

8

Watch carefully and see if you can tell me exactly what happens to a ball:

a. As we throw and catch it (it is pushed from one hand to another pair of hands).

b. When I drop it (it moves from a high place to a low place).

Watch one of the birds on a lawn carefully. See if
you can map where it moves as it changes its position.

How can you see over the wall? (By climbing up on
a chair.)

Can you map the movements of somebody playing in
the children's playground?

9

Which way does the postman go to deliver letters
in your street? Does he go in the same direction every
day?

Where do we hope our hot-air balloon will go when we
release it?

Describe the directions of movements of:

Leaves blown from trees in autumn.
Fruits and seeds attached to plumes.

Use the position of numbers on the clock face for
describing the directions of children's movements.
For instance, to reach the tree shown on the right

George must move towards 7 o'clock.
Mary must move towards 5 o'clock.

Concept: compass directions

We will all go outside to find out where the sun is at
12 noon today. From where we are standing we are
looking towards the south. North, east and west may
also then be indicated from the same point.

From which compass direction must the wind come
to push the arrow on the weather vane to point south
or in another given direction?

Use compass points to describe the position of:

The sun at different times of the day.
The direction in which the stick's shadow points.
The position of landmarks seen during outdoor
expeditions.

4 Out and about with young children

Now it may be helpful to see what happens to children when they work with teachers who make use of ideas such as those given in the previous chapters.

When a teacher is alive to the opportunities that any moment of the day can present, the beginning will be very simple and spontaneous. For example, the headmistress of a large infant school noticed a six-year-old boy outside her window watching a plastic bag he was gently waving to and fro. He had been sent outside to collect some soil for a classroom activity but his attention had been distracted when he held up his bag in the air, found it filling out and felt the resistance as he tried to draw it downwards. He was observing and thinking about these things when he was seen. As a result of the ensuing conversation he returned to his classroom with the soil but also with a number of ideas he wished to try out with a plastic bag of air.

Then there was the six-year-old who strayed from the PE lesson to examine a pattern in the mud left by a tractor lumbering towards the school building extensions. In response to his interest, the class teacher, and others who had gathered round, were soon agreeing that the V-shapes in the mud were like roof shapes upside down or corners of triangles on their Mathematics Table.

This was how the class began to make a collection of V-shaped patterns from the surrounding housing estate. They also started pressing objects on to different materials in an attempt to discover more about making patterns in the same manner as the tractor—and incidentally much more also about the hardness and softness of different materials.

Open french doors to classrooms, freedom to move in and out of school grounds where a variety of things grow and change, will make these spontaneous conversations and activities possible.

V-shaped patterns in the mud left by a tractor

Making an impression of a footprint in the mud

One afternoon in May a few years ago I went for a walk 'down the lane' with the teacher and class of twenty-eight six- to seven-year-old children from a rural school. We wished to find out what would arouse their interests and lead to conversation.

For this class the walk was a new experience and the children's first response before leaving their playground was vigorous running around. They began by enjoying the freedom of movement in the larger spaces. Gradually they gathered by the gate and were then ready to set off.

The first source of genuine interest was a large machine mowing the grass in the recreation ground by the side of the school. There was discussion about the driver of the machine, the way it was turned round, reasons for cutting the grass and the shortness of what was left. Turning their backs on this, the children looked at a field of growing corn and some noticed that this was like grass but growing in rows rather than all over the ground. Some children were interested in plants by the roadside; we collected some and compared their heights. Others responded to a suggestion that they might look for different kinds of leaves. Looking around and standing still to listen led to conversation about the hum of the telegraph wires, and then they began listening for other sounds and discussing their causes, until somebody pointed out the vicar's house in the distance and his TV aerial.

Then a move was made past the school and headmaster's house to the church. We looked up at its tower and the weather vane. The comments of children who had noticed that this could face in different directions made them look around for more effects of the wind. They found movement in the washing on the line in the headmaster's garden and in the long grass between the graves in the churchyard, and a coolness on their faces when they faced in a certain direction.
Then in response to a boy's remark about the flints in the churchyard wall, the children felt the material between the flints, the church gate and the tombstones, and words for describing these tactile sensations were suggested. Their interest in materials persisted as they moved along the lane because a number of cottages of wood and stone, different in colour and shape, came into view. Some children again began hunting for spring flowers by the hedge and this time they wanted names for their finds. As we came to the ruin of a Home-Guard shelter where metal rods protruded from the broken concrete wall, there was plenty of conversation about this metal and the thickness of the wall, and some children referred to the way men mix concrete. There was some discussion about the reasons for things being strong.

Soon after this we reached the end of the lane where it opened out to some waste ground facing a wide expanse of water where two river estuaries met. In response to suggestion the children began to look around and upwards and downwards and name all the things they could see moving, but after a time they concentrated their interest on the boats travelling up and down the river. The fact that only some had sails was noted and there was general agreement that the wind moved these boats along. Some wondered whether

further use and comparison. When they stood still we encouraged them to wonder about natural phenomena such as rain, clouds and wind.

As soon as we returned to the classroom an empty desk was covered with kitchen paper and on this the children began to set out their flowers and leaves in small jars. This was completed by the end of the afternoon, but during the days which followed the children made much use of some well-illustrated books about wild flowers, and some names, discovered by matching real flowers with pictures, were printed on cards and added to the display.

Following up the Nature Walk

the wind made the waves and ripples on the water. One child suggested that boats might move more quickly if they went the same way as the water moved. While this discussion proceeded some children resumed their search for wild flowers.

Another small group began to talk about the sky because they were interested in a very black cloud in the distance with streaks of rain falling from it and the contrasting clear blue sky on either side. This soon attracted the attention of most of the children and interest developed rapidly. There were many questions. Can clouds turn into rain? Are clouds made of water? Is that cloud turning into water? Will the cloud go when all the rain has fallen? Why does the rain fall downwards? Will it ever rain when there are no clouds in the sky?

The return journey to the classroom followed the same pattern but took place more rapidly for the children had satisfied their curiosity about much of the route.

An outdoor world such as this, providing so much to see and examine, is complex and the teacher's role in using an experience of this type is vital. We knew the route well and so did many of the children, but during the hour spent out of doors we tried to help them to see as they looked around at different levels and we encouraged them to make use of more than one of their senses. They collected materials, flowers and leaves for

The arrangement and rearrangement of this material gave rise to much thought and conversation. During the following days the walk provided inspiration for many drawings, paintings and freely written work.

Their drawings were interesting. Some were based entirely on experiences during the walk, while others also included the children's memories of more distant experiences. This was especially the case with the older children. One boy's view of the mower on the recreation ground included details of machinery inside the bonnet, possibly remembered from a picture once seen or the experience of watching his father work on the family car.

These drawings also revealed considerable differences in the children's awareness of the position of one object in relation to another. One child's drawing of the church was quite flat, while a boy of the same age produced a very good impression of the vicarage and its TV aerial, partly concealed from the road by trees and a hedge.

The children's ideas of the size of one thing in relation to another also varied widely, while their written work differed in length from two or three lines to a page. It is very important to notice these degrees of understanding in the children, for they indicate to the teacher the kind of help that children need next.

The church has a sign of North South East and West on the tower.

We saw some of the tombstones in the churchyard.

When I returned to the class a week later I produced a drawing of the road to represent the route of the walk and the children selected some of their pictures to mount on either side of this. Finally, with a thick pen, I wrote in some of the sentences from their written work between their pictures. The final result was a long frieze telling the story of the expedition and when this was placed along the wall it served as a reading aid and subject for discussion. The remaining pictures and written work were mounted in a class book and hung next to the frieze. This was frequently consulted and shown to visitors who came to the school.

I found the horses most interesting.
One was a male and the other a
female. They were both brown and
white in colour. The female seemed
to want to stay in the background
but the male come forward and even
tried to chase some boys. The small
field they were in was surrounded by
a fence.

Children of seven to nine years in the neighbouring class soon became aware of the activities of the younger children and they too explored the lane. When their frieze is compared with that produced by the younger group we have some interesting illustrations of the children's progression.

This was only the beginning of going out for these children. When towards the end of the term I visited that class again I found the children had been spending much time with their teacher on the waste ground near the river, but on these occasions their interest had been concentrated on the ground. There was no book or

Between the farm and the beach there was a field with some ducks in. Mr Breden said they could go to swim in the pond by the from farm. It was cloudy.

frieze. The flowers had vanished from the table covered with kitchen paper and instead there were three tables extending along one complete side of the classroom. On one was set out a large collection of pebbles and stones and the name of the colour of each one had been written by the children on the kitchen paper. On the next table some pebbles had been grouped according to size, others according to shape. The children had found out that different oval and round stones could be flat or spherical and that oval stones could break in halves transversely and longitudinally, though they did not use these words in describing their discoveries to me.

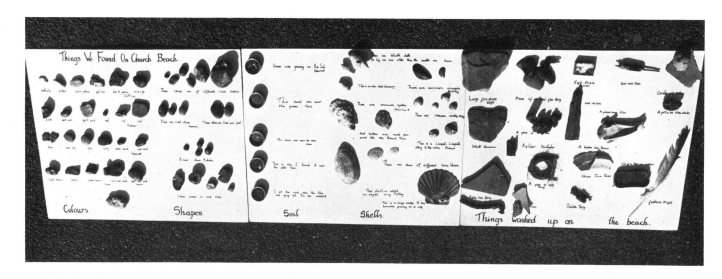

Things We Found On Church Beach

Colours   Shapes

Soil   Shells

Things washed up on the beach.

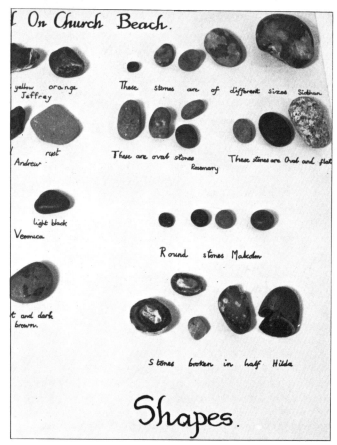

l On Church Beach.

yellow   orange
Jeffrey

rust
Andrew

Light black
Veronica

t and dark
brown.

These   stones   are   of   different   sizes   Sidhan

These are oval stones
Rosemary

These stones are Oval and flat

Round   stones   Malcolm

Stones   broken   in   half   Hilda

Shapes.

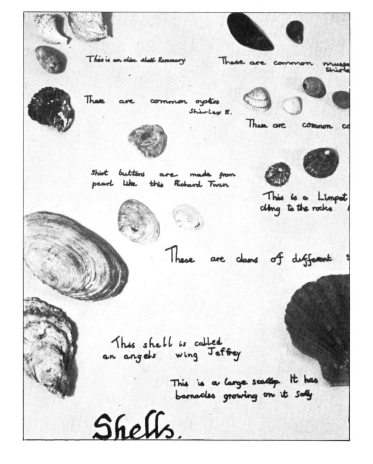

This is an olive shell Rosemary   These are common muss
Shirle

These   are   common   oysters
Shirley E.

These   are   common   c

Shirt buttons are made from
pearl like this Richard Twin

This is a Limpet
cling to the rocks

These   are   clams   of   different

This shell is called
an angels wing Jeffrey

This is a large scallop It has
barnacles growing on it Sally

Shells.

74

Large fire stone Nigel

Pieces of coloured glass Barry

Egg Shell Peter

Bul- rush Julia

Cardboard Lesley

Wad Helen

A pieces bone Kim

A potato MALCOLM

A piece of cork John

Slate Eamonn

Rubber Christopher

A broken tile Richard

Lid of a Meat can Siobhan

China Tina Owen

Arrow shaped flintstone David Blackwell

A piece of rope Penny

feathers Nigel

Rusty iron Barry

Pottery Alan

Onion Terry

Things washed up on the beach.

The third table contained the results of beachcombing. Objects such as bones, a coconut shell, china, tin lids, plastics, rubber and leather were named, again on the kitchen paper, according to the material of which they consisted. The children had much to tell me about this effort for they were so proud of it, and it was obvious that they had sorted the items in their collection very carefully in order to produce it. At the same time there had been thinking about colours, shapes, sizes and the textures of materials.

This all took place six years ago, but only two weeks before writing this account a girl approached me when I was visiting a secondary school, introduced herself as a member of the expedition to the river and was delighted to learn that the story of the walk and the collection of stones were still in my possession.

The writing of this child in her last term in the infant school is evidence of the inspiration that can come from sensory experience out of doors.

'At half past one we went out for a sound walk. I heard the birds singing above my head. We stamped our feet and made soft and loud noises and when we walked and ran on the grass we made quiet sounds and when we got nearer the woods we stopped and listened. The leaves were making loud rustling noises. There were lots and lots more leaves in the woods and that is why the sound was louder. We then walked on the stones. The stones went click, click, that is because you knock each other when you walk on them. We picked up two stones and we played Humpty Dumpty. It was not a pleasant sound. The stones just go click, click. Piano sounds are nicer as it has high and low noises.

'Then we all stamped our feet on the playground. We made a noisy sound thump, thump, thump. Miss Kite's sandals only made a soft little sound, the boys' shoes made the loudest noise, a lot of the boys had leather soles and that is why it was so loud. Sounds on the grass are soft when we jumped, skipped and ran on the grass we discovered the sound was quieter. When we heard an aeroplane over our heads it made a loud noise, a growing twig won't crack but a dead twig does. When the aeroplane went further and further you couldn't hear it!'

Writing does not give the complete picture. Many of these young children's communications about their sensory experiences are oral and therefore difficult to collect. When one teacher wrote down as many of the comments of the six-year-old children in her class as she could manage, while they were collecting and examining pebbles on the seashore near some chalk cliffs, I was able to make the following analysis of the words relating to the stones they found.

Colour

White	Green	
Blue	Mauve	
Orange	Black	
Yellow	Pink	
Grey	Brown	
Red		

Size and shape

Pointed	Enormous
Bumps	Lines
Solid	Bobble
Big	Heavy
Straight	Patterns on it
Flat	Holes in it
Spikes	Dented
Tiny	

Appearance and texture

Pretty	Sharp
Shiny	Attractive
Rough	Bumpy
Smooth	Horrible
Ugly	Dirty
Beautiful	

Similes

Hard like a rock	Rolls like a ball
Half a sausage	Like an apple
Shape of a pear	Like a shoe
Shell like	Like a bean
Like a puzzle	Like a diamond
Like a ball	Like a pea
Like an egg	Shaped like a jet
Like ice cream	

In another class of six-year-old children I found there had been a search around the neighbourhood in their own time for things with interesting scents. The lists on the classroom wall revealed their opinions about the discoveries they had made and also an early attempt to form two sets of the things observed.

Smells I like	Smells I dislike
Nail varnish	Crabs
Bath crystals	Fly spray
Powder puff	Paint
Roses	Manure
Lavender	Moth balls
Scent	Washing-up water
Sausages	Pond weed
Strawberry jam	Fish
Soot	Oil
Toothpaste	Petrol *
Petrol *	Onions
Oranges	Smoke
Pansies	Tar *
Sweets	
Hair cream	
Fish and chips	
Tar *	

*Means that children's opinions were divided.

It seems that children begin to compare their discoveries at an early age. In an urban school situated just behind a busy shopping centre I found that the five-year-old children, nearing the end of their first term in the reception class, had been encouraged to look on the ground in their own gardens for stones and pebbles and these were spread out in great abundance on a large table together with a strip of wood. I had the following conversation with a small boy who brought the wood from the table to show me. He rubbed one stone along the wood and said : 'I can make a stripe.' When I inquired how that was done he selected from the table a flint with a very sharp edge and made a mark on the wood. When I asked why the stone made a stripe he showed me the flint and at the same time running his finger along its side said : 'Because it's sharp.' Then I asked whether he had any stones that would not make a stripe and he selected a round pebble and demonstrated its lack of effect on the wood.

He said little more and used no words such as blunt or smooth. He could say nothing about the hardness of the wood or stones. Through trials with these materials he had found a way of comparing the flint and the pebble and was aware of certain differences between them. But he could not relate his experience to the correct words, so the communication of his knowledge was through motion with real objects rather than language.

Another group of children forming the reception class of a village school also became interested in noticing the difference between things. When men came to repair the roof of the church near their school they took to wandering from their classroom to the playground railings to watch and make friends with the workmen.

The smoke blew in our playground It made our eyes sting. We could smell it in school.

Some workmen came to our church. They pulled off the roof.

A gift of wood from the old roof, riddled with tunnels made by death-watch beetles, encouraged their discussions, and they searched in picture books to see where other animals made their homes. One day the workmen made a bonfire with beams from the old church roof and the children's ability to smell and look and feel soon helped them to discover more about the differences between smoke and air.

Some time later, undeterred by memories of smarting eyes, acrid smell and tickling throats, the children were eager to go with their teacher across to a corner of the churchyard to rake among the cold ashes from the

When the bonfire went out, we went to see what we could find.

bonfire, and their curiosity was rewarded by the discovery that wood when burnt could become two different things: grey powdery ashes and black lumps of material with which they could mark and draw.

They also discovered that the bonfire did not change the old nails that had held beams of the roof together for hundreds of years; these they found, still bent and rusty, lying in the ashes. Although they were pleased with their discoveries and displayed them prominently in the classroom they accepted the differences they found and showed no interest in the reasons.

We found wood-ash, charcoal, and nails.

Instead, their attention turned again to the men at work, now mixing concrete to fix new roof beams in place, and they tried to mix a gift of sand and cement too. Later, however, as the repair work approached completion, their interest in fire and its effect was renewed. One was lit beneath a boiler to heat lumps of asphalt. They saw these solid lumps going into the boiler and were very interested in the thick black stream that was eventually poured out. Through these first observations of burning and melting they had much to say about what fires can do.

A boiler stood outside our school.
The workmen melted asphalt in it.
They took the asphalt up to the roof
and poured it over the concrete.
Now our church has a new roof.

Seven-year-old Michael who was an intelligent boy went much further than this. The Nature Table was a source of great interest to the members of his class because each child was encouraged to make self-chosen contributions to it. Michael specialised in soils. His specimens (entirely of his own choice, found around his home) were all contained in equal-sized glass screw-top jars through which the colours showed well. Each jar was just over three-quarters full and this enabled him to compare the soils by looking at their colours, handling them, holding the jars containing roughly the same volume and listening to the sounds produced as they were shaken. These were all Michael's own ideas for examining his materials and he brought his screw-top jars from home. This is an extract from the book he made to go on the table with his specimens.

'Chalk
This chalk came from the cliffs of Pegwell Bay. This chalk is white if you shake it it breaks and it becomes powder.

'Pebbles
These pebbles come from Deal beach when you shake them they do not break they make a noise.

'Builder's Sand
Builder's sand is in lumps but when you shake the san it breaks and it makes a soft noise.

'Sand
When you shake this sand it makes a ratteling sound because it has little bits of grit in it.

'Wet Sand
Wet sand is hard and it is heavy and it stuck to my fingers when I shake the bottle it did not move but dry sand did.

'Leaf Mould
Leaf mould is hard and light it stuck to my fingers and is dark and nearly black with little lumps.'

When Michael wished to find out more about his soils, he was able to draw from much more past experience than the younger children and so was able to think of many more things to do to give him the information he wanted. He took care to treat each specimen in the same way so that the differences between them emerge clearly in his recording. The only help he required from his teacher was interest and appreciation. Many children of the same age with less intelligence and initiative would have needed more assistance than Michael in making some sort of examination of their materials, and even he was not ready to wonder why the differences he had discovered existed.

In this chapter the activities of children between the ages of five and seven years have been described, for it is right that this work should begin in the infant school. But there will be many junior and secondary school teachers who will receive children from classes where the outdoor surroundings have not been used as part of the everyday environment. For them many ideas in this book may offer appropriate starting points, for an idea can be used with children of any age.

What will vary will be the way the children will respond, the depth to which they will pursue an investigation, the skill and degree of accuracy they will bring to bear on their tasks, and the speed with which they find particular things on which to concentrate more attention and so progress to more comprehensive studies.

Some further suggestions for organisation of outdoor work

Different circumstances in schools will bring about differences in the way outdoor work must be organised, but as so much value is attached to conversation and discussion any arrangements should be designed to give children easy access to adults with some understanding of their needs.

Outdoor investigations can form part of any normal school day when children can move easily and informally to well-designed school grounds (Volume 4, Chapter 1) and their teacher can go outside quite frequently to give help to individuals.

When two or three teachers work together in a team-teaching situation it is possible to achieve greater variety in the size of groups and sometimes allow one teacher to take a few children (eg ten) for a field expedition.

A more complex organisation is required when it is necessary to work with a whole class beyond the school premises. The following suggestions are relevant to such situations.

Study areas
The most suitable places to visit will be those where children can wander and probe without danger or damage to property. These areas need not be large. If possible they should be within easy walking or travelling distance so that return visits can be made.

Timing
Fieldwork should take place at all seasons of the year. Frequent short expeditions for different purposes provide better learning situations than occasional long, tiring outings into which a wide range of experiences are crowded. Suitable periods would be 10-45 minutes in the school grounds, and between one hour and half a day farther afield.

Contact with adults
Generous adult/child ratios can be obtained by enlisting the help of:

Interested parents.
Students from a college of education.
Older boys and girls from secondary schools concerned with studies of child development.

Small working groups each with an adult leader can be formed.

Before setting out
The teacher should:

a. Make proper arrangements for access if entry to a nature reserve or private property is involved.

b. Visit the study area, if possible with assistants.

c. Hold a briefing meeting for assistants to give information about the site and discuss objectives and ways of working and the types of conversation likely to be helpful.

d. Acquaint children with general arrangements but withhold any information they can discover at first hand on the site.

On the site

On arrival it is advisable to:

Select a place for depositing coats, bags, etc.
Indicate boundaries of the study area.
Give a signal to be used for recalling groups (eg whistle).

Working groups can then disperse to pursue exploratory activities.

Care of the countryside

The following should be avoided:

Unnecessary collecting; destruction of rare plants; trampling on vegetation; damage to trees, hedges and walls.

Everyone should be reminded to shut gates and keep to footpaths near crops.

This, as well as the safety precautions below, should be learned through practice of good habits in the field.

Safety precautions

These should include:

a. Kerb drill or application of the Green Cross Code at busy roads.

b. Avoiding tasting things.

c. Use of plastic bags and containers for specimens rather than glass jam jars and bottles.

The teacher should carry a small first-aid kit and know the position of the telephone nearest to the study area.

'Follow-up' on return

Children who enjoy outdoor work will wish to share their experiences, and this is the incentive for much useful follow-up work. This should be *personal* work, for children will be attracted by different aspects of their surroundings and they will wish to make use of various materials in communicating their ideas.

Those who have a lot to say or are too young to write much will enjoy using a tape recorder. Others will need paints and fabrics, modelling and writing materials or squared paper. Some children will need longer than others to think about the visit before they are ready to produce anything.

Therefore materials should be freely available in the classroom at all times so that children can fit this work into their daily programmes whenever it seems right to do so.

Work likely to be produced:

Tape recordings of conversations, descriptions and early poems.
Pictures that can be mounted to form friezes.
Large murals (co-operative efforts).
Models in clay.
Illustrated books containing factual descriptions (these would contain contributions from all members of the class).
Individual illustrated booklets (children six to nine years old).

Addendum: Pupils' units

Since this book was first published, the *Learning Through Science* project, which followed the *Science 5/13* project, has produced a series of pupils' assignment cards, arranged in 12 thematic packs, each with its own Teachers' Guide. The two packs that particularly relate to the work discussed in the present book are *All Around* and *Out of Doors*. The *Learning Through Science* pupils' units are also published by Macdonald.

Objectives for children learning science

Guide lines to keep in mind

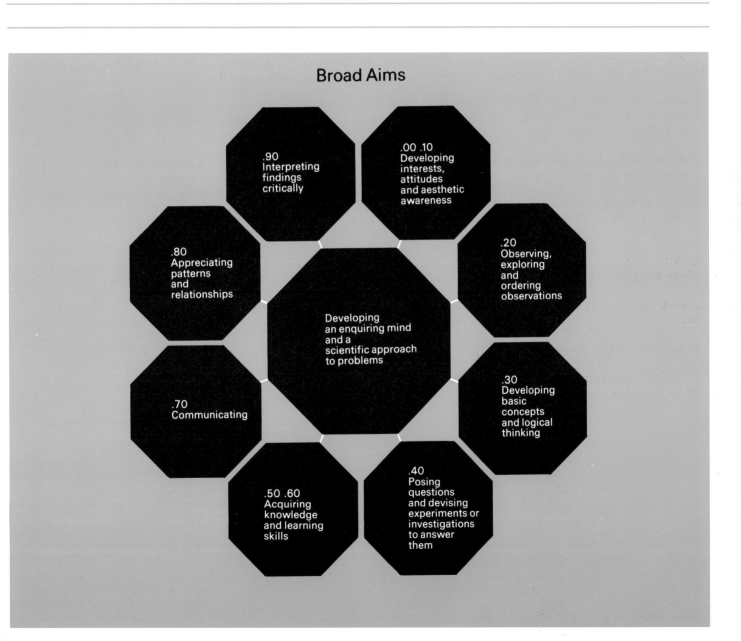

Broad Aims

.90 Interpreting findings critically

.00 .10 Developing interests, attitudes and aesthetic awareness

.80 Appreciating patterns and relationships

.20 Observing, exploring and ordering observations

Developing an enquiring mind and a scientific approach to problems

.70 Communicating

.30 Developing basic concepts and logical thinking

.50 .60 Acquiring knowledge and learning skills

.40 Posing questions and devising experiments or investigations to answer them

What we mean by Stage 1, Stage 2 and Stage 3

Attitudes, interests and aesthetic awaren

.00/.10

Stage 1
Transition from
intuition to
concrete
operations.
Infants
generally.

The characteristics of thought among infant children differ in important respects from those of children over the age of about seven years. Infant thought has been described as 'intuitive' by Piaget; it is closely associated with physical action and is dominated by immediate observation. Generally, the infant is not able to think about or imagine the consequences of an action unless he has actually carried it out, nor is he yet likely to draw logical conclusions from his experiences. At this early stage the objectives are those concerned with active exploration of the immediate environment and the development of ability to discuss and communicate effectively: they relate to the kind of activities that are appropriate to these very young children, and which form an introduction to ways of exploring and of ordering observations.

1.01 Willingness to ask questions
1.02 Willingness to handle both living and non-living materi
1.03 Sensitivity to the need for giving proper care to living things.
1.04 Enjoyment in using all the senses for exploring and discriminating.
1.05 Willingness to collect material for observation or investigation.

Concrete
operations.
Early stage.

In this Stage, children are developing the ability to manipulate things mentally. At first this ability is limited to objects and materials that can be manipulated concretely, and even then only in a restricted way. The objectives here are concerned with developing these mental operations through exploration of concrete objects and materials—that is to say, objects and materials which, as physical things, have meaning for the child. Since older children, and even adults prefer an introduction to new ideas and problems through concrete example and physical exploration, these objectives are suitable for all children, whatever their age, who are being introduced to certain science activities for the first time.

1.06 Desire to find out things for oneself.
1.07 Willing participation in group work.
1.08 Willing compliance with safety regulations in handling tools and equipment.
1.09 Appreciation of the need to learn the meaning of new words and to use them correctly.

Stage 2
Concrete
operations.
Later stage.

In this Stage, a continuation of what Piaget calls the stage of concrete operations, the mental manipulations are becoming more varied and powerful. The developing ability to handle variables—for example, in dealing with multiple classification— means that problems can be solved in more ordered and quantitative ways than was previously possible. The objectives begin to be more specific to the exploration of the scientific aspects of the environment rather than to general experience, as previously. These objectives are developments of those of Stage 1 and depend on them for a foundation. They are those thought of as being appropriate for all children who have progressed from Stage 1 and not merely for nine- to eleven-year-olds.

2.01 Willingness to co-operate with others in science activit
2.02 Willingness to observe objectively.
2.03 Appreciation of the reasons for safety regulations.
2.04 Enjoyment in examining ambiguity in the use of words.
2.05 Interest in choosing suitable means of expressing resul and observations.
2.06 Willingness to assume responsibility for the proper care living things.
2.07 Willingness to examine critically the results of their ow and others' work.
2.08 Preference for putting ideas to test before accepting or rejecting them.
2.09 Appreciation that approximate methods of comparison be more appropriate than careful measurements.

Stage 3
Transition to
stage of
abstract
thinking.

This is the Stage in which, for some children, the ability to think about abstractions is developing. When this development is complete their thought is capable of dealing with the possible and hypothetical, and is not tied to the concrete and to the here and now. It may take place between eleven and thirteen for some able children, for some children it may happen later, and for others it may never occur. The objectives of this stage are ones which involve development of ability to use hypothetical reasoning and to separate and combine variables in a systematic way. They are appropriate to those who have achieved most of the Stage 2 objectives and who now show signs of ability to manipulate mentally ideas and propositions.

3.01 Acceptance of responsibility for their own and others' safety in experiments.
3.02 Preference for using words correctly.
3.03 Commitment to the idea of physical cause and effect.
3.04 Recognition of the need to standardise measurements.
3.05 Willingness to examine evidence critically.
3.06 Willingness to consider beforehand the usefulness of th results from a possible experiment.
3.07 Preference for choosing the most appropriate means of expressing results or observations.
3.08 Recognition of the need to acquire new skills.
3.09 Willingness to consider the role of science in everyday

Attitudes, interests and aesthetic awareness

.00/.10

Observing, exploring and ordering observations

.20

1.21 Appreciation of the variety of living things and materials in the environment.
1.22 Awareness of changes which take place as time passes.
1.23 Recognition of common shapes—square, circle, triangle.
1.24 Recognition of regularity in patterns.
1.25 Ability to group things consistently according to chosen or given criteria.

1.11 Awareness that there are various ways of testing out ideas and making observations.
1.12 Interest in comparing and classifying living or non-living things.
1.13 Enjoyment in comparing measurements with estimates.
1.14 Awareness that there are various ways of expressing results and observations.
1.15 Willingness to wait and to keep records in order to observe change in things.
1.16 Enjoyment in exploring the variety of living things in the environment.
1.17 Interest in discussing and comparing the aesthetic qualities of materials.

1.26 Awareness of the structure and form of living things.
1.27 Awareness of change of living things and non-living materials.
1.28 Recognition of the action of force
1.29 Ability to group living and non-living things by observable attributes.
1.29a Ability to distinguish regularity in events and motion.

2.11 Enjoyment in developing methods for solving problems or testing ideas.
2.12 Appreciation of the part that aesthetic qualities of materials play in determining their use..
2.13 Interest in the way discoveries were made in the past.

2.21 Awareness of internal structure in living and non-living things.
2.22 Ability to construct and use keys for identification.
2.23 Recognition of similar and congruent shapes.
2.24 Awareness of symmetry in shapes and structures.
2.25 Ability to classify living things and non-living materials in different ways.
2.26 Ability to visualise objects from different angles and the shape of cross-sections.

3.11 Appreciation of the main principles in the care of living things.
3.12 Willingness to extend methods used in science activities to other fields of experience.

3.21 Appreciation that classification criteria are arbitrary.
3.22 Ability to distinguish observations which are relevant to the solution of a problem from those which are not.
3.23 Ability to estimate the order of magnitude of physical quantities.

	Developing basic concepts and logical thinking **.30**	**Posing questions and devising experiments or investigations to answer them** **.40**
Stage 1 Transition from intuition to concrete operations. Infants generally.	*1.31* Awareness of the meaning of words which describe various types of quantity. *1.32* Appreciation that things which are different may have features in common.	*1.41* Ability to find answers to simple problems by investigati *1.42* Ability to make comparisons in terms of one property or variable.
Concrete operations. Early stage.	*1.33* Ability to predict the effect of certain changes through observation of similar changes. *1.34* Formation of the notions of the horizontal and the vertical. *1.35* Development of concepts of conservation of length and substance. *1.36* Awareness of the meaning of speed and of its relation to distance covered.	*1.43* Appreciation of the need for measurement. *1.44* Awareness that more than one variable may be involved a particular change.
Stage 2 Concrete operations. Later stage.	*2.31* Appreciation of measurement as division into regular parts and repeated comparison with a unit. *2.32* Appreciation that comparisons can be made indirectly by use of an intermediary. *2.33* Development of concepts of conservation of weight, area and volume. *2.34* Appreciation of weight as a downward force. *2.35* Understanding of the speed, time, distance relation.	*2.41* Ability to frame questions likely to be answered throug investigations. *2.42* Ability to investigate variables and to discover effective ones. *2.43* Appreciation of the need to control variables and use controls in investigations. *2.44* Ability to choose and use either arbitrary or standard units of measurement as appropriate. *2.45* Ability to select a suitable degree of approximation and work to it. *2.46* Ability to use representational models for investigating problems or relationships.
Stage 3 Transition to stage of abstract thinking.	*3.31* Familiarity with relationships involving velocity, distance, time, acceleration. *3.32* Ability to separate, exclude or combine variables in approaching problems. *3.33* Ability to formulate hypotheses not dependent upon direct observation. *3.34* Ability to extend reasoning beyond the actual to the possible. *3.35* Ability to distinguish a logically sound proof from others less sound.	*3.41* Attempting to identify the essential steps in approachin a problem scientifically. *3.42* Ability to design experiments with effective controls for testing hypotheses. *3.43* Ability to visualise a hypothetical situation as a useful simplification of actual observations. *3.44* Ability to construct scale models for investigation and appreciate implications of changing the scale.

Acquiring knowledge and learning skills

.50/.60

1.51 Ability to discriminate between different materials.
1.52 Awareness of the characteristics of living things.
1.53 Awareness of properties which materials can have.
1.54 Ability to use displayed reference material for identifying living and non-living things.

Acquiring knowledge and learning skills

.50/.60

1.55 Familiarity with sources of sound.
1.56 Awareness of sources of heat, light and electricity.
1.57 Knowledge that change can be produced in common substances.
1.58 Appreciation that ability to move or cause movement requires energy.
1.59 Knowledge of differences in properties between and within common groups of materials.

1.61 Appreciation of man's use of other living things and their products.
1.62 Awareness that man's way of life has changed through the ages.
1.63 Skill in manipulating tools and materials.
1.64 Development of techniques for handling living things correctly.
1.65 Ability to use books for supplementing ideas or information.

2.51 Knowledge of conditions which promote changes in living things and non-living materials.
2.52 Familiarity with a wide range of forces and of ways in which they can be changed.
2.53 Knowledge of sources and simple properties of common forms of energy.
2.54 Knowledge of the origins of common materials.
2.55 Awareness of some discoveries and inventions by famous scientists.
2.56 Knowledge of ways to investigate and measure properties of living things and non-living materials.
2.57 Awareness of changes in the design of measuring instruments and tools during man's history.
2.58 Skill in devising and constructing simple apparatus.
2.59 Ability to select relevant information from books or other reference material.

3.51 Knowledge that chemical change results from interaction.
3.52 Knowledge that energy can be stored and converted in various ways.
3.53 Awareness of the universal nature of gravity.
3.54 Knowledge of the main constituents and variations in the composition of soil and of the earth.
3.55 Knowledge that properties of matter can be explained by reference to its particulate nature.
3.56 Knowledge of certain properties of heat, light, sound, electrical, mechanical and chemical energy.
3.57 Knowledge of a wide range of living organisms.
3.58 Development of the concept of an internal environment.
3.59 Knowledge of the nature and variations in basic life processes.

3.61 Appreciation of levels of organisation in living things.
3.62 Appreciation of the significance of the work and ideas of some famous scientists.
3.63 Ability to apply relevant knowledge without help of contextual cues.
3.64 Ability to use scientific equipment and instruments for extending the range of human senses.

Communicating	Appreciating patterns and relationships
.70	**.80**

Stage 1
Transition from
intuition to
concrete
operations.
Infants
generally.

1.71 Ability to use new words appropriately.
1.72 Ability to record events in their sequences.
1.73 Ability to discuss and record impressions of living and non-living things in the environment.
1.74 Ability to use representational symbols for recording information on charts or block graphs.

1.81 Awareness of cause-effect relationships.

Concrete
operations.
Early stage.

1.75 Ability to tabulate information and use tables.
1.76 Familiarity with names of living things and non-living materials.
1.77 Ability to record impressions by making models, painting or drawing.

1.82 Development of a concept of environment.
1.83 Formation of a broad idea of variation in living things
1.84 Awareness of seasonal changes in living things.
1.85 Awareness of differences in physical conditions betw€ different parts of the Earth.

Stage 2
Concrete
operations.
Later stage.

2.71 Ability to use non-representational symbols in plans, charts, etc.
2.72 Ability to interpret observations in terms of trends and rates of change.
2.73 Ability to use histograms and other simple graphical forms for communicating data.
2.74 Ability to construct models as a means of recording observations.

2.81 Awareness of sequences of change in natural phenom
2.82 Awareness of structure-function relationship in parts c living things.
2.83 Appreciation of interdependence among living things.
2.84 Awareness of the impact of man's activities on other ∎ things.
2.85 Awareness of the changes in the physical environmen brought about by man's activity.
2.86 Appreciation of the relationships of parts and wholes.

Stage 3
Transition to
stage of
abstract
thinking.

3.71 Ability to select the graphical form most appropriate to the information being recorded.
3.72 Ability to use three-dimensional models or graphs for recording results.
3.73 Ability to deduce information from graphs: from gradient, area, intercept.
3.74 Ability to use analogies to explain scientific ideas and theories.

3.81 Recognition that the ratio of volume to surface area is significant.
3.82 Appreciation of the scale of the universe.
3.83 Understanding of the nature and significance of chang in living and non-living things.
3.84 Recognition that energy has many forms and is conser when it is changed from one form to another.
3.85 Recognition of man's impact on living things— conservation, change, control.
3.86 Appreciation of the social implications of man's chang use of materials, historical and contemporary.
3.87 Appreciation of the social implications of research in science.
3.88 Appreciation of the role of science in the changing pattern of provision for human needs.

Interpreting findings critically

.90

1.91 Awareness that the apparent size, shape and relationships of things depend on the position of the observer.

1.92 Appreciation that properties of materials influence their use.

2.91 Appreciation of adaptation to environment.
2.92 Appreciation of how the form and structure of materials relate to their function and properties.
2.93 Awareness that many factors need to be considered when choosing a material for a particular use.
2.94 Recognition of the role of chance in making measurement and experiments.

3.91 Ability to draw from observations conclusions that are unbiased by preconception.
3.92 Willingness to accept factual evidence despite perceptual contradictions.
3.93 Awareness that the degree of accuracy of measurements has to be taken into account when results are interpreted.
3.94 Awareness that unstated assumptions can affect conclusions drawn from argument or experimental results.
3.95 Appreciation of the need to integrate findings into a simplifying generalisation.
3.96 Willingness to check that conclusions are consistent with further evidence.

These Stages we have chosen conform to modern ideas about children's learning. They conveniently describe for us the mental development of children between the ages of five and thirteen years, but it must be remembered that ALTHOUGH CHILDREN GO THROUGH THESE STAGES IN THE SAME ORDER THEY DO NOT GO THROUGH THEM AT THE SAME RATES.
SOME children achieve the later Stages at an early age.
SOME loiter in the early Stages for quite a time.
SOME never have the mental ability to develop to the later Stages.
ALL appear to be ragged in their movement from one Stage to another.
Our Stages, then, are not tied to chronological age, so in any one class of children there will be, almost certainly, some children at differing Stages of mental development.

Index

Illustration acknowledgements:

The publishers gratefully acknowledge the help given by the following in supplying photographs on the pages indicated:

Barnaby's Picture Library, Photographer: Ken Lambert, 10 left
British Airports Authority, 52 left
British Waterways Board, Photographer: Derek Pratt, 69 left
D. F. Clayton RIBA, County Architect, Kent, 53 left, 62 left
East Malling Research Station Studio, 45 right
Greater London Council, 45 left
E. P. Hicks, 5
P. I. Howes, 30
Kent Messenger, 54 right, 60, 62
Medway College of Design, 77, 78
Mervyn Rees, 15 right, 19, 21, 29, 31, 58, 59, 61, 74, 75
National Farmers' Union Library, Photographer: John Topham Limited, 42
Standard Oil Co. (NJ), 15 left

All other photographs by kind permission of W. H. Petty MA, BSc, County Education Officer, Kent, Photographer: M. Williams
Line drawings by Eleanor Mills
Cover design by Peter Gauld